BBC

AS guru

General Studies

**Alyson Boustead, Fiona McMillan,
Ian Ford and David Goldblatt**

Published by BBC Educational Publishing, BBC White City,
201 Wood Lane, London W12 7TS.

First published 2001

Reprinted in 2001

© Alyson Boustead, Fiona McMillan, Ian Ford and David Goldblatt

Colour reproduction, printed and bound by Sterling press, Northamptonshire.

ISBN 0 563 54236 5

To place an order, please telephone Customer Services on 0870 830 8000 (Monday – Friday, 0800 – 1800)
or write to BBC Educational Publishing, PO Box 234, Wetherby, West Yorkshire, LS23 7EU.

Visit the BBC Education website at: www.bbc.co.uk/education

Contents

Culture, morality, arts and humanities 7

Religions 8

Morality 10

Aesthetics 12

Culture 14

Classical music 16

Popular music 18

Theatre 20

Cinema 22

Literature 24

Modern art 26

Advertising 28

Television news 30

Practise questions 32

Maths 33

Number, shape and space 34

Algebra 40

Statistics 42

Functions and graphs 44

Probability 48

Algorithms and networks 50

Practice questions 52

Science and technology 53

What is science? 54

Evolutionary theories 56

Evolution and creation 58

Climate change 60

Natural hazards 62

Energy: fuels 66

Energy: the nuclear debate 68

Energy: Sizewell and the future 70

Sustainability and Agenda 21 72

Genetics and cloning 74

Cloning and research 76

Genetically engineered crops 78

GE food: forming the argument 80

GE food: what does the future hold? 82

Practice questions 84

Society, politics and the economy   **85**

    Values in society   86

    Values today   88

    The UK political system   90

    UK political parties   94

    The UK Welfare State   98

    The National Health Service   102

    Law and ethics   106

    Crime: the death penalty   108

    Crime: prison   110

    The European Union   112

    Globalisiation   114

    The poverty gap   116

    The legacy of colonialism   118

    International debt and international aid   120

    Arguments about international aid   122

    Practise questions   123

Answers   **124**

Glossary   **134**

Introduction

GURU TIP

Tip boxes like this appear throughout the book to give you good ideas and hints about maths.

Many of you will not have studied General Studies before, so you may be wondering what it's all about and what benefit there is in studying it. The BBC AS Guru™ materials aim to answer these questions and guide you through the labyrinth that is AS General Studies. AS Guru™ includes:

- this book • a website • TV programmes.

These elements complement each other and provide lots of information, inspiration and practice questions to give you a thorough grounding in General Studies.

AS General Studies aims to help you broaden your knowledge of life and develop a wide range of skills at the same time. More specifically you will:
- develop a greater awareness of human knowledge, understanding and behaviour;
- understand the historical and contemporary contexts of issues and use these to develop your skills of evaluation
- use knowledge from a range of subjects and an understanding of how they relate
- examine issues from several sources and standpoints, reviewing strengths and weaknesses
- solve problems using different approaches and justifying the ones you chose
- use your knowledge to build clear and convincing arguments in an appropriate format and style.

What is General Studies about?

GURU TIP

Domain: a field or scope of knowledge.

AS General Studies is about everything that affects the way you live. Most General Studies specifications are divided into 3 subject domains:
- culture, morality, arts and humanities
- science, mathematics and technology
- society, politics and the economy.

If the thought of learning about all this seems overwhelming – don't panic! You will be using lots of knowledge that you already have or have access to, for example:

- you have recently studied up to ten subjects at GCSE, which address some of the subject matter in each domain so you should have a basis of transferable knowledge of many of the subjects to bring to AS General Studies.

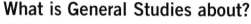

GURU TIP

Any words that appear in bold, in the text, are important ones to understand. The definitions of these words can be found in the glossary at the back of the book.

- you can use the work you are doing in your other AS level subjects, as AS General Studies gives you the opportunity to use this knowledge.
- you will need to become more critically aware of what effects these domains have on life in the 21st Century.
- You'll be tested on issues of current interest, so it's important that you're aware of what's going on in the news.

You can use the AS Guru™ materials as your guide. It's not possible to cover every topic about life, so what AS Guru™ does is:

- outline some of the major issues of the times within each domain
- give you a wide range of viewpoints to help you develop your own
- provide you with starting points and ideas for further study
- give you tips on study skills and skill building throughout each section.

Information boxes like this give you extra facts and details you should know.

What skills will you need for AS General Studies?

You'll need to take responsibility for your own learning, making sure that you research and understand the issues. Important skills to develop are listed below.

- **Communication** – you will be assessed on your ability to express complex ideas clearly and intelligibly so that anyone can understand them;

- **Awareness** – you should keep informed of current developments by regularly reading a quality newspaper and a selection of relevant magazines, such as *The Economist*, *New Scientist* and the *Times Literary Supplement*; watch documentaries, current affairs and news programmes, such as *Newsnight* and *What the Papers Say*; listen to radio programmes, such as *Today*; research background information on topics using both the library and the Internet.

- **Exemplification** – use topical examples of issues to back up your points wherever necessary.

- **Analysis** – critically explore a range of different viewpoints about issues, weighing up which is the most convincing and then convince an examiner how and why you reached your conclusions.

What's in it for you?

Apart from gaining some useful UCAS points, AS General Studies will provide:

- knowledge of a wide range of thought-provoking and controversial topics
- the ability to develop and express your own opinions, to understand and appreciate different viewpoints and to raise your awareness of modern issues
- a wider perspective on issues that occur both in AS General Studies and your other AS Level subjects
- evidence for your key skills portfolio (see more about this on page 6)

How is General Studies assessed?

AS General Studies is examined through three assessment units, one per module, which can be taken in January or June. If you underachieve in a module examination you can re-sit it once and the higher score will stand.

Each paper utilises a range of different types of questions in order to assess different abilities and skills. You will come across the following types of questions:

Short answer questions – which involve the analysis of and response to stimulus material, for example a newspaper article, some data or an advert.

Multiple choice question – which provide you with several answer options that you must choose from.

Essay writing – which involves writing in response to a question or stimulus material. These essays may vary in length from approximately 200 to 500 words, so you need to practise doing both types.

Quality of written communication

You will also be marked on your ability to:

- write in a manner appropriate to the purpose
- organise information clearly and using appropriate vocabulary
- write neatly and use accurate spelling, punctuation and grammar.

GURU TIP
You don't have to know everything about everything. Examiners are more interested in your thinking and analytical skills than how much subject content you can regurgitate.

GURU TIP
Make sure you understand the key words regularly used in essay questions – look up the following in a good dictionary:

**compare contrast
define describe
discuss explain
illustrate justify
outline relate
review state
summarise trace**

Essay structure is important. A good, argumentative essay will:

- have an introduction that defines key terms of the question and explain what will be covered

- the main body of the essay, which sets out both sides of the argument

- a conclusion which attempts to balance both viewpoints, or comes down in favour of one over the other.

Key skills

By now, you may be familiar with the term Key Skills. These are skills you are expected to develop over your AS/A2 studies, which will make you highly desirable to future employers and universities. There are six Key Skills, but only three contribute to the Key Skills qualification. They are:

- Application of Number
- Communication
- Information Technology

To gain a Key Skills qualification, you need to collect a portfolio of evidence, which is like a folder of coursework compiled from your AS/A2 subjects, to show your ability to fulfil certain criteria (see below); you may also sit terminal examinations (although some subjects you take at A2 level will 'let you off' this, for example, if you complete an A Level in English you will be exempt from the terminal exam in Communication).

General Studies will provide plenty of opportunities to produce evidence of attainment in all Key Skills. Although it will largely be up to your teacher or lecturer to give you clear opportunities to fulfil Key Skill requirements, the responsibility for building up a strong portfolio will be on you. To help you, in this book, opportunities to put Key Skills into practice and gather evidence for your portfolio throughout your AS General Studies course, are flagged up.

The chart below shows you the skills you must demonstrate in the three main Key Skills areas, and what's required to fulfil each one. You should be aiming to meet the criteria laid down for level 3.

C3	**Communication level 3**
C3.1a	Contribute to a group discussion about a complex subject.
C3.1b	Make a presentation about a complex subject, using at least one image to illustrate complex points.
C3.2	Read and synthesise information from two extended documents that deal with a complex subject. One of these documents should include at least one image.
C3.3	Write two different types of documents about complex subjects. One piece of writing should be an extended document and include at least one image.
N3	**Application of number level 3**
N3.1	Plan, and interpret information from two types of sources including a large data set.
N3.2	Carry out multi-stage calculations to do with: amounts and sizes; scales and proportion; handling statistics and rearranging and using formulae. Work with a large data set on at least one occasion.
N3.3	Interpret results of your calculations, present your findings and justify your methods. You must use at least one graph, one chart and one diagram.
IT3	**IT level 3**
IT3.1	Plan and use different sources to search for, and select, information required for two different purposes.
IT3.2	Explore, develop, and exchange information and derive new information to meet two different purposes.
IT3.3	Present information from different sources for two different purposes and audiences. Your work must include at least one example of text, one example of an image and one example of numbers.

Culture, morality, arts and humanities

In this section you will learn about:

☞ conflicts between high culture and popular culture

☞ effects of the media

☞ the role of religion and morality

☞ how all of these topics link together in one domain.

AS General Studies aims to teach you about life and would not be complete without a section on culture, morality, arts and humanities. This is because the subjects covered – religion, morality, aesthetics, culture, music, theatre, cinema, literature, art and the media – play a major part in the social and personal lives of all people in British society.

You will already know quite a bit about all of the subjects in this domain:

* you may be studying arts- or humanities-based subjects amongst your AS levels
* you will probably enjoy popular culture and may appreciate high culture too
* you are part of a highly media-literate generation
* you may participate in creative, musical or artistic pursuits and/or practise a faith
* you are living in a multicultural and multi-faith society
* you will have had to make some difficult decisions and have a point of view on certain controversial issues.

Your prior knowledge and experiences are highly valuable, because in AS General Studies, you are welcome to express your own ideas and viewpoints. As long as you remember that, in an exam, balanced and truthful answers which show an understanding of both sides of an argument will score higher than passionate but personal diatribes. Therefore, this section sets out to focus some of your ideas and provide you with a framework to hang them on.

The key to your success in AS General Studies is developing a point of view about everything! Some people find this harder to do than others, but it'll get easier with practise. Even if you find that you cannot decide what you should think about a topic after you've explored both sides, as long as you show an understanding of what issues are at stake, you will succeed.

As you read this section:

* make sure you understand both sides of every argument
* think about how it may affect you
* watch news programmes and read quality papers and magazines
* research issues you are not sure about on the Internet or in the library
* always ask yourself 'What do I think about this issue?'

Religions

Britain is a multicultural and multi-faith society and religious education is a compulsory subject in schools, so it's no surprise that it has a place in AS General Studies. You will all have studied religion previously at school and so you may be expected to know about the variety of religions and beliefs practised in this country. This topic looks at what religion in general has achieved and the major religions of the world.

- **Judaism:** the religion of the Jews, based on the Old Testament of the Bible and the Talmud and having a central belief in one God as the creator of all things and the source of all righteousness.

- **Islam:** the religion of Muslims, having the Koran as its sacred scripture and teaching that there is only one God and that Mohammed is his prophet.

- **Hinduism:** the system of beliefs, values and customs that are the dominant religion in India and are characterised by the worship of many Gods, belief in reincarnation and a caste system.

- **Buddhism:** the religious teaching spread by the Buddha and his followers, which preaches that man can achieve perfect enlightenment by destroying greed, hatred and delusion, since these are the causes of all suffering.

- **Christianity:** the religion whose believers follow the teachings of Jesus Christ.

What does religion achieve?

- **Social control:** religion not only underpins the unwritten rules about how you should live your life, for example saying that you should not commit adultery, but also supports written laws, by forbidding crimes such as murder and theft. You could argue, therefore, that religion teaches the basic morality that allows people to understand the difference between right and wrong. Religion also exerts a certain amount of social control by promoting ideas that make people act in a civilised manner. For example, it supports the protection of the individual against lawlessness and promotes the concept of forgiveness by re-admitting sinners and those who have broken the written laws to society.

- **Individual identity:** according to social anthropologist Bronislaw Malinowski, religion gives meaning to life. At certain stages in their lives, people often question who they are, why they are here, what purpose they have and why their loved ones have to die. These questions cannot be addressed logically or scientifically, but religion can provide the answers.

- **Social change:** churches and the clergy have supported various worthy causes that aimed to improve life for others. Examples include:

  – fighting for civil rights for all races

  – helping to abolish slavery

  – playing a vital part in prison reform.

- **Social life:** religious gatherings comfort the lonely by providing an opportunity for them to meet others and also promote community feeling. Malinowski maintains that religion also offers the comfort and support that the bereaved need to cope with a death in the family. Others think that sharing the beliefs of a religion brings people together. Religious services, such as those held on Remembrance Day, remind them of their common beliefs and values.

KEY SKILLS
To fulfil the requirements for Key Skill IT3.3, write a report and produce a PowerPoint presentation about whether religion has a future in Western society. After your first draft ask your tutor and your peers for advice on how to improve your presentation and revise what you have done in the light of their comments.

Bronislaw Malinowski was an anthropologist, who explored magic and religion, testing his hypotheses in the field.

He helped define the roles of science and myth in society.

See p9 for a discussion about how the decline in influence of Christianity and our increasingly multifaith culture are affecting our moral beliefs.

> **Research focus:** should religious organisations become involved in what might be considered political causes? Should they confine themselves to spiritual matters or do they have a duty to bring about social change? What do you think? Try to read about and discuss these ideas and develop your own viewpoint.

What are the negative consequences of religion?

- **Conflict:** religious beliefs can lead to violence and even major conflicts. For this reason, many people believe that religion does more harm than good. The ongoing troubles in Northern Ireland and Israel have their roots in religious conflict.

> **Research focus:** can you think of any more conflicts in which religious differences play a part? What is the present-day situation in Chechnya and in Afghanistan? Historically, what caused the Thirty Years War? Find out by following the newspapers and looking up the causes of past conflicts so that you have the basic facts and arguments to hand.

- **Prejudice:** religion can not only cause **bigotry** and intolerance on a large scale, but also at the level of the individual. Ignorance and a lack of understanding about the beliefs of others can lead to irrational **prejudices**. Moreover, people within religious groups who do not conform or question the validity of the faith may suffer **persecution** or be **ostracized** as a result.

- **Conservatism:** religion can be seen as an essentially **conservative** institution that prevents change or progress. It has also supported reactionary governments in the past. For example, the Roman Catholic church has been accused of co-operating with the Italian fascists in the 1930s and during World War II.

- **Exploitation:** Karl Marx, the 19th Century thinker and revolutionary, believed that religion supported the rich and powerful and exploited the working classes. He claimed that religion is the 'opiate of the people' because it numbs the hardships they suffer during life with the expectation of rewards in the afterlife. As a result, the oppressed accept their fate instead of fighting for change. Marx also believed that religious belief keeps the powerful classes in power by justifying their privileges. For example, in Victorian times Christians believed that the way the world was arranged was God's will and could not be changed. This idea legitimised class barriers and prevented attempts to change society.

> Do the advantages of religion outweigh the disadvantages? Can a balance be struck between the certainty of your beliefs and tolerance towards those of others? Is religion an engine for social change or repression? What do you think?

Is religion being replaced in this country?

There is no doubt that the number of people practising religion was much higher at the beginning of the 20th Century than it is now, but why is this? It could be said that because of great advancements in scientific knowledge and technology that allow us to explain and understand more about the world, people don't rely on religion for answers. Moreover, Western society seems to be driven more by materialism than spiritualism. Religion is a powerful force in many people's lives but, as society progresses, will religion in the UK survive to see the beginning of the 22nd Century?

Culture, morality, arts and humanities

> **GURU TIP**
> The topic of religion can inspire strong opinions. Feel free to express your own views but always remember that a balanced and truthful argument, which shows that you understand all viewpoints, will score more marks than a personal diatribe for, or against religion.

GURU WEBSITE
Visit the AS Guru™ website at:

www.bbc.co.uk/asguru

for a discussion on different attitudes towards religion.

Morality

Many of the issues covered in the General Studies syllabus revolve around whether the arguments for and against them are considered moral – whether they involve right or wrong, or good or bad behaviour. In order to answer questions on these issues you will need to understand the concept of **morality** and explain why and how you have arrived at the views you hold. But what does the word '**moral**' mean? This is one definition, from *Collins English Dictionary, 1991:*

> Moral *adj.* **1.** concerned with or relating to human behaviour, esp. the distinction between good and bad or right and wrong behaviour: moral sense. **2.** adhering to conventionally accepted standards of conduct. **3.** based on a sense of right and wrong according to conscience: moral courage; moral law.

Morality is the knowledge and practice of what is moral, which may, according to your personal view:
- be instinctive
- be associated with religion and culture
- be acquired by reasoning.

You will almost certainly have some ideas about what you believe to be right and wrong. You will probably have been encouraged to give reasons for acting and behaving in a certain way.

Sometimes the reasons are obvious: certain actions are against the law, which means that society has decreed the actions to be morally wrong, and sometimes common sense says they are wrong. For example, murder is illegal, but instinct and practical judgement tell you that it is wrong in any case.

At other times, your decisions about right and wrong may be based on the consequences of your actions. You will consider in what way your actions would affect others and yourself, and whether the effects justify the actions.

When you are unsure whether an action or behaviour is right or wrong (it may be unclear what the consquences to yourself or others will be), you are faced with a moral dilemma. In order to discriminate between right and wrong, you must make a moral judgement. It is moral judgements that affect the way you think about certain issues and make you act in certain ways.

> **Research focus:** how did you develop your views on right and wrong in the first place? Was it because you believe in a higher authority, such as a holy text, that tells you how to behave? Was it because of how you have been brought up and influenced by the beliefs of those closest to you? Have you conformed to the expectations of your culture? Once you have analysed why you think as you do, you will find it easier to justify your views.

Moral philosophy

Moral philosophy – sometimes referred to as **ethics** – deals with human conduct and can help you to put up a logical defence of your feelings about right or wrong. The discipline has evolved over the centuries, but it originated with the work of Greek philosophers Socrates, Plato and Aristotle.

- **Socrates** (469–399 BC) believed that virtue is based on knowledge that is acquired through a reasoned debate informed by a stated hypothesis.
- **Plato** (429–347 BC) believed that by living virtuously your life will be made happy and morally correct.
- **Aristotle** (384–322 BC) believed that happiness should be the ultimate product of all human action and that virtuous actions are essential for well-being and happiness.

This section looks into some examples of the ideas behind moral philosophy.

- **Divine command theory:** if you adhere to this theory, you believe that killing, stealing, causing injury and so on are immoral because such acts are forbidden in religious writings and are against your God's will. In other words, you believe that you should live life according to the rules laid down in a religious work.

- **Emotivism:** this theory suggests that moral judgments are not made universally. When you make statements about what you feel is morally wrong, whether it be genetic engineering or homelessness, all you are doing is expressing a personal feeling that has been triggered by your emotions.

- **Natural law:** argues that people are all linked by a common humanity and it is part of human nature to live according to moral principles. To have ideas about natural justice and rights is a natural product of being human.

- **Situationism:** suggests that the only thing that makes an act right or wrong is the presence or absence of love. Love is the one thing in the world that is completely good and defines the difference between good and evil.

- **Utilitarianism:** is the doctrine that morality is all about securing the maximum happiness for the maximum number of people. Behaviour is moral when its consequences are good more often than bad.

- **Intuitionalism:** suggests that you all have intuitions that lead to common sense judgments about what is right and what is wrong, and that if your motives for action are to bring about something good then you cannot be morally wrong.

- **Kantianism:** a theory formulated by Immanuel Kant, who thought that a moral action defines itself and is something that is good in its own right. He believed that you know naturally what is right because this is a universal law. Kant called this the categorical imperative.

- **Existentialism:** opposed to Kantianism, this theory argues that there are no universal rules and that as individuals you have to invent your own rules. Individuals choose a course of action and in doing so, exhibit what they believe to be their own morals.

Research focus: find out what contribution these famous thinkers made to the debate about morality:

- Thomas Aquinas (1225–1274)
- Thomas Hobbes (1588–1679)
- Jeremy Bentham (1748–1832)
- John Stuart Mill (1806–1873)
- Immanuel Kant (1724–1804)
- Friedrich Nietzsche (1844–1900).

Try the Internet, encyclopaedias and philosophy books for information.

KEY SKILLS
Use different IT sources to find out about the listed philosophers and about current topical moral issues.

This research could be the basis for fulfilling the criteria for Key Skill IT3.

GURU TIP
Collect material on a current affairs moral issue that interests you. As a revision aid:

- **define** the issue
- **examine** why it arouses such strong feelings
- **explore** a range of different viewpoints
- **outline** your personal views, giving reasons for them and using the theories of moral philosophy to back up your arguments.

Culture, morality, arts and humanities

Some moral dilemmas facing society in the 21st Century are covered later in this book. See page 78 for information on genetic engineering. Moral beliefs are discussed in the Values in society section on page 86.

Aesthetics

Have you ever used the phrase 'aesthetically pleasing' before and, if so, what were you talking about? The chances are that you were referring to something that was pleasing to look at. But the study of **aesthetics** is not restricted to this. It is the philosophical study of beauty and taste in all branches of 'the arts' – a collective term for all the imaginative, creative and non-scientific branches of knowledge. So anything that can be described as beautiful, including music and literature, can be said to be aesthetically pleasing. In AS General Studies, an understanding of the ideas behind aesthetics will help you to talk critically in an exam about the arts and formulate ideas about what makes a work of art.

How can you judge what is beautiful and what is not? It isn't difficult to make a list of things that you find aesthetically pleasing, but it is harder to justify your view. It is not so much a question of whether you are right or wrong, but on what you base your opinion. In this **context**, and according to one school of aesthetic judgement, your personal feelings and responses are perfectly valid. Here are two definitions and a quote that are worth remembering:

> - **Objective** – having views that are not distorted by personal bias
> - **Subjective** – having views that are influenced by personal feelings
>
>   'Actually I do not think that there are any wrong reasons for liking a statue or a picture.' EM Gombrich, in *The Story of Art* (Phaidon Press)

Aesthetic judgements

There are two main ways of looking at an object to decide whether it has aesthetic value. Use these concepts to help you justify your views about what has aesthetic value and what does not:

1 **State of mind:** this is the subjective justification, in that an object can be considered aesthetically pleasing if it pleases the admirer and gives a feeling of satisfaction – 'beauty is in the eye of the beholder'. For example, you may reasonably admire a picture or enjoy a passage from a novel because it reminds you of something – a place that has sentimental memories or a person you know and like. However, it may not have the same appeal for someone else.

2 **Conceptual understanding:** this is the objective justification. It is an academic approach that assesses what is aesthetically pleasing by using a set of rules that justifies how objects should be understood and evaluated. The rules are:
- in order to evaluate an object's aesthetic value, the admirer must have knowledge about its genre, who created it and its social, cultural and historical background
- the admirer must also apply a set of conceptual rules to the study of the object to decide whether or not it has aesthetic value.

By this justification, when you find a sonnet by Shakespeare aesthetically pleasing it is because:
- you know about the social, historical and cultural period in which it was written
- you are aware of Shakespeare's preoccupations at the time of writing
- it conforms to the strict structure, rhythms and rhymes of the sonnet form
- it has appropriate subject matter and can be analysed using the rules of literary criticism.

Ask yourself whether a work you find aesthetically pleasing appeals primarily to your subjective emotions or, objectively, conforms to a set of conceptual rules. Do you think you can only appreciate a piece of music by Schubert, say, if you have prior knowledge of its form and its relevance to musical thought?

Ways of looking at the arts

There are many ways to view art in order to decide what the aesthetic qualities are:

- **As a sensory experience.** Art may appeal to your senses through sight, hearing or imagination. A piece of music, for example, may move you.

- Through **symbolism.** Art may use symbolic images. Such symbols contain messages about the way the artist sees the subject and can reflect the social and historical context in which the work was produced. For example, in his 1945 novel *Animal Farm,* George Orwell uses pigs to symbolise capitalists.

- Through **representation.** An artist interprets an aspect of reality. A work may faithfully represent the appearance of a real subject – an example is a portrait that is aesthetically pleasing because it is so accurate – or it may try to describe something that you cannot see, such as the artist's inner feelings or comments on society. Picasso's *Guernica* (1937), for example, is a protest against fascism.

- Through **expression.** The artist may not produce a clear representation of a subject but portray it in a unique way – an example being the work of abstract artist Jackson Pollock (1912–1956). You may find that this kind of art is much more difficult to understand because it doesn't relate to an interpretation of reality.

- Through **form.** You may take pleasure from the style, arrangement and design of a piece of art rather than its content. For example, a novel, a sonnet and a sonata all have a fixed form and mode of expression to which they must conform in order to achieve success and give the piece meaning.

To assess the aesthetic value of a piece of work you must also take current trends and tastes into account. These change over time. Compare the designs and shapes that were popular in the 1960s, '70s and '80s, with what is considered popular now. Think of buildings, such as revolutionary state-of-the-art housing estates. For example, Hulme, in Manchester, was seen as being at the cutting edge of design in the 1960s but was demolished as a disaster in the '90s. Some designs are regarded as classics and never go out of fashion, such as the Mona Lisa, painted by Leonardo Da Vinci. Use the Internet and resources at your town or college library, to find other design examples that have stood the test of time, and some that haven't lasted as long.

You can aesthetically assess anything that gives you pleasure. Take popular music for example. Most of you will listen to it and enjoy it every day and you might have definite ideas about what kind of music you prefer. Many of you will be able to evaluate exactly why you enjoy it. Remember to use recognised and accurate musical terms and show that you understand why certain music appeals to you when you articulate your appreciation (see page 16 for some terms to get you started).

You could aesthetically evaluate how people present themselves. How a person ornaments themselves is a starting point. Think about jewellery, tattoos, piercings and make-up. You could develop the evaluation by analysing how these decorations construct the identity of the person by altering their body and making them different to other people. Body decoration, scarring, body painting, tattooing and dressing are central to self-construction and spiritual life in all cultures.

GURU TIP
Use your textbooks or the Internet to look up these names and research the study of aesthetics further:

Aristotle
Immanuel Kant
Arthur Schopenhauer

GURU TIP
A musical analysis will sound more convincing if you can relate your discussion in terms of sociology, psychology or social anthropology.

Culture

GURU TIP
Use the following pages on topics such as music and art to develop your point of view on aspects of high culture and popular culture.

What do you mean by the term 'culture'? You will have come across it regularly during your AS General Studies course, but do you really understand it? The term can be used in several contexts, some of which are listed below.

- **Common culture:** any set of inherited or derived beliefs, values, ideas and knowledge that are shared by certain groups within society. For example, young people are often said to have a common culture, which is referred to as 'youth culture'.

- **National culture:** the traits that are seen to be peculiar to a nation. For example, in Britain, events such as the Changing of the Guard or a football Cup Final could be said to be part of our national culture.

- **High culture:** the works of writers, artists and composers who are considered by scholars and critics to be superior to others. This culture is associated with the educated and affluent who can both understand it and afford to take part in it. High culture includes appreciation of:
  – writers, such as Shakespeare and Dickens
  – composers, such as Purcell and Elgar
  – artists, such as Constable and Gainsborough.

- **Popular culture:** the opposite of 'high culture', also known as 'low culture', being the works of writers, artists and composers who are considered to appeal to a mass audience from all areas of society. Popular culture is mainly a product of the late 20th Century and embraces forms of entertainment that have mass appeal, such as:
  – television shows
  – the cinema
  – popular music.

The culture debate

Admirers of high culture believe it has more worth than popular culture because:

- it has aesthetic and intellectual value that can be pondered over, forever
- it is 'true art' that has been produced alone, often in defiance of current **convention** and in a pre-industrial way.

They attack popular culture because:
- it is easy to understand and designed for instant pleasure, with no requirement to think long or hard about its meaning
- it is designed primarily to make money, concentrating on attracting mass audiences rather than creating something of value
- it concentrates on arousing the more basic instincts in humans, such as an obsession with sex and violence, and does not promote refined qualities
- popular culture involves industrial production and, like the output of a factory, is repetitive and does not allow artists scope to express themselves properly
- it is dull and mundane, reflecting the lives of the majority of the audience (who are also assumed to be generally dull and mundane)
- it reflects the further 'dumbing down' of society.

But does popular culture really have so little worth? Many people believe that it is valuable and use the arguments on the next page to support their belief.

- Not all popular culture is meaningless or easy to understand. Many examples incorporate complex ideas, make demands on the audience's imagination and intellect and command fine performances by the participants. For example, some Hollywood films are thought-provoking and appeal to your emotions, and certain soap operas can skilfully convey the seriousness of an issue to a mass audience.
- Most of the criteria used to assess the value of high art forms can also be used to evaluate popular art forms: music theory has analysed popular music; literary criticism has analysed tabloid articles and Hollywood movies; theses have been written about sitcoms and soap operas.
- Not all popular entertainment is driven by profit. Some bands aren't manufactured by record companies and make music to reflect their ideas and feelings.
- Over generations, ideas about what is considered high culture and what is considered popular culture often change. For example, many of Shakespeare's plays were originally written for commercial gain and to entertain the masses as much as the nobility, but now they are regarded as classics. Do you think the same will happen to the popular music of today?
- High culture is elitist and deliberately excludes people, whereas popular culture involves everyone. Entertaining the masses for the same cost of entertaining an elite few is a fairer and better use of resources.
- Finally, a product that aids relaxation and offers some kind of gratification at the end of a hard working day surely has value.

So where do you stand in the culture debate? You may well be asked this question in your exam, with reference to a particular form of culture, such as painting or music. It may be easier to talk about the merits of high culture, but it is equally valid to defend popular culture if you have a sound basis for your argument.

National culture

Many aspects of our culture can be seen as typically British, but Britain is becoming increasingly multicultural as it embraces culture from other countries. Reasons for this range from the fact that more people can choose to work and live in different countries and take part of their culture to that country, to **globalisation** (see page 114), which is spreading Western culture to the rest of the world. Britain no longer has a **monoculture** (one culture) and is increasingly **multicultural**.

On the other hand, perhaps there are certain things that make you feel particularly British, and these things combine both high culture and popular culture, for example:

- when you sing the National Anthem or hear the hymn *Jerusalem*
- when you read literature such as Dickens, Austen and Shakespeare
- if you support British football teams
- when you drink tea, eat fish and chips and talk about the weather!

If these make you feel proud to be part of this culture then you could be said to believe in **nationalism**, which is a sentiment based on common cultural characteristics that bind a population together. There are negative connotations associated with nationalism because of groups, such as The National Front who believe that Britain is superior to all other cultures. However, this is a narrow interpretation. Britain is sometimes accused of having a nationalist, 'island mentality' and this is used as one of the reasons why it isn't fully integrated in the European Union (see page 112). Do you think it is right for a country to retain feelings of Nationalism or is time the world began to think of itself as a 'global community'?

GURU TIP
Assess the popular culture that surrounds you – use specific examples in an exam. Ask yourself:

- what gratification do they offer?
- do they have value?
- could you defend them in a debate on high culture versus popular culture?

KEY SKILLS
Lead a group discussion on the culture debate, initiating the discussion. Listen and respond sensitively to the ideas of others.

This could contribute towards achieving Key Skill C3.1a.

Culture can be defined in many ways. This section has concentrated on culture in the media, but there are many elements that define our national culture. These include, the Arts, race, the multicultural nature of the UK, religion, language and the Monarchy.

Think hard about what makes up the national culture of the UK.

KEY SKILLS C3.1a

Classical music

In order to answer a General Studies question that involves classical music, you need to be familiar with a number of composers and their work. The examiners want to see that you have a considered and objective approach and that your answer is balanced and based on fact as well as opinion. You may need to:

- justify why classical music has more longevity than popular music
- communicate your awareness of the creative process
- interpret two versions of the same piece of music
- compare popular and classical music
- explain what classical music means to people and why they enjoy it.

What does music mean?

Before the 19th Century, most orchestral music was abstract. Choral music and opera, for example, have always had very specific meanings, and were used to portray stories, information and emotion. This form of music was called **absolute music**. Mozart's concertos, for example, created a sense of feeling but each phrase formed part of the whole picture, rather than being able to stand on their own as a statement. Around 1800, a form of music, called **programme music**, came to light. This way of composing enabled each portion of a piece of music to be broken down to a literal meaning; it tried to depict objects and events. The idea that music could mean something was around long before this time but it was about the time of Beethoven (1770–1827) that programme music formed the majority of all classical music. Academic debate about these ideas exists between two different schools of thought: the **referentialists** and the **non-referentialists**.

Non-referentialists

This school of thought, sometimes called formal or absolute, believes that:

- music exists alone and has no extra-musical associations
- music is an art of intrinsic principles and ideas
- the elements of music – harmony, melody and rhythm – are only meaningful to each other and to the way that they work together to create a certain sound
- music is not symbolic of anything else.

Non-referentialists would say that if you listened to Saint-Saëns' *Carnival of the Animals* (1886), for example, you would find it hard to recognise that the musical phrases denote animals, without knowing the title. They believe that this shows that people enjoy music because of its sound alone and not because of what it might mean.

Referentialists

Referentialists believe that:

- music is like language and can therefore be used to produce statements
- composing music is like using words to express yourself
- music is capable of communicating feelings and ideas
- music can refer to objects that exist outside of music and is said to have extra-musical associations when it does.

Referentialists would say that *Carnival of the Animals* contains musical phrases that could evoke images of the suggested animals, and that one of the reasons why people enjoy music is the associations it evokes.

No matter which school of thought you agree with, it is obvious that different listeners derive different meanings from the same piece of music. What they are may depend on a listener's life experiences, knowledge and taste in music, and when the piece is heard.

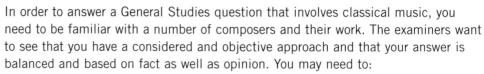

GURU TIP

When you tackle a question about music it's important to use the correct terms. Here are some of them, but it is a good idea to research more.

Melody – the key ingredient of any piece of music, which may be the tune or the most distinctive arrangement of notes.

Harmony – the arrangement of notes that supports the tune and produces complementary sounds.

Rhythm – the beat, which gives music pace and timing.

Tone – the quality, pitch and volume of music

Mood – emotions or feelings that a piece of music can evoke.

The Russian composer Dmitri Shostakovich (1906–1975) said: 'Music alone is powerless to evoke anything'. Do you agree? Where do you stand in the debate between the referentialists and the non-referentialists? Find a piece of music to back up your arguments, such as Mendelssohn's *Fingal's Cave*.

Culture, morality, arts and humanities

What happens when you listen to music?

Much of the enjoyment you experience when listening to music is created by the wide range of emotions and associations that it evokes. Music can stimulate both your mind and your senses by powerfully evoking memories, suggesting moods and triggering emotions. This power comes from the mixture of sounds and silence that works at a deep level of consciousness. The tone and pace of a piece can also help to create these effects. For example, minor keys can evoke discontent, lively rhythms can suggest excitement and cascading strings may indicate romance. Certain instruments have historical associations that help to evoke particular ideas. For example:

- the flute was traditionally played by Pan, the ancient Greek god of shepherds and flocks, and can evoke pastoral images of shepherds and country life
- the trumpet is associated with battle and can sound martial
- the harp has connotations of angelic and ethereal images, while the violin represents the voice of the devil.

How to work out what you think

Bearing in mind what happens when you listen to music, work through these steps to help formulate you own ideas about the value of classical music.

- Find a piece of classical music that you enjoy and listen to it.
- Do some research on it and find out the social, historical and cultural background of both the music and its composer. Does this knowledge alter your ideas and enjoyment of the piece or does it give it any special significance?
- Does the music mean anything, either to the composer or to you?
- Think hard about what else may make you enjoy the piece. For example, does it remind you of a person or place that holds strong memories for you? Does it rouse any emotion in you, such as happiness or sadness? Do you particularly like the sounds of certain instruments?
- Discuss its musical qualities. Does it, for example, have appropriate pace, a memorable melody, a rhythm designed for dancing or a pleasing harmony?

When you have gone through this exercise, ask yourself whether you enjoy the piece as much or more than a piece of popular music? If so, why? If not, why not?

Choose your words carefully

Try not rely on terms like 'great', 'brilliant' or 'amazing' to describe music in your AS examinations. Learn to break musical compositions down (both classical and popular) into their basic ingredients: melody, harmony, rhythm, mood and form (see the Guru tip on the opposite page) and plan your essays around these terms.

GURU TIP

It is worth researching different styles of music so that you can quote examples in your answers. Here are a few to start you off:

Baroque (c.1700) – produced dignified and courtly music, such as Bach's *Brandenburg Concerto*.

Classical (c.1750) – produced balanced and restrained sounds, such as Mozart's *Piano Concerto No 21*.

Romantic (c.1900) – was cerebral, unrestrained and even melodramatic – Liszt's *Les Préludes*, is an example.

Popular music

The first thing that comes to mind when you think about popular culture is likely to be pop music. Like it or loathe it, it is part of people's everyday lives: at home, on television, on the radio at work and over loudspeakers in shopping centres. Pop music is an integral part of modern culture, so it is useful to develop your views about it. In your General Studies exam you could, for example, be asked whether pop music has as much integrity as classical music, or whether it will become the 'classical' music of the future.

A brief history of pop music

The 1950s marked the beginning of the pop music industry. Its birth coincided with the growing popularity of television, the establishment of popular radio stations, technological advances and the phenomenon known as 'the teenager'. During this time, young people had more money and more freedom than ever before, and they became the new industry's target audience.

Young, attractive stars were plucked from obscurity and groomed for success. Predominantly, they played rock 'n' roll, a musical genre that originated as a blend of rhythm and blues, and country and western. Meanwhile, merchandise, clothing and magazines devoted to the stars proliferated, so that teenagers could participate in the experience that pop music offered them. It gave them an image that expressed their new-found status in society and emphasised their rebellion against the conservative values of post-war adulthood.

> In the 1950s, when the term 'teenager' was first used, popular music was both a revolutionary movement and an expression of freedom for the newly influential youth culture. Can you say the same about pop music today?

What gives pop music its mass appeal?

The music itself
Pop music can evoke feelings in the same way as classical music. For example, a melody in a minor key can portray sadness and one in a major key can inspire elation. However, unlike classical music, pop music can be more easily interpreted because pop songs have lyrics that indicate the singer's feelings and allow listeners to relate them to their own worlds.

Usually, pop music lyrics are short stories that dramatise the ups and downs of life, sung by the singer as if they have lived through the events in person and cleverly summed up in a catchy chorus. Some artists cash in on their very 'public' personal experiences – examples include 'Tell Me', Mel B's anthem to her divorce, and George Michael's confessional 'Fast Love'. In other cases, the songs are specially created by professional songwriters.

Mass-produced emotion this may be, but as long as every generation of the target audience continues to experience both the pleasure and pain of human life and the pop industry taps into both, pop music will remain hugely popular.

The image
Have you ever thought that you might like a particular type of music because of the image and lifestyle that goes with it? A variety of tastes, attitudes and cultures are represented by the pop industry and there are a variety of identities to go with them.

GURU TIP
Develop your arguments and collect quotes by reading the music press, and the arts pages of broadsheet newspapers, which carry detailed music reviews.

GURU TIP
Whatever your view on popular music, you will have to justify it to an examiner. Be prepared to back up your opinion with quotes, facts, figures and a convincing argument.

This means that becoming a fan of a particular style of music has a social function because it allows people to conform with their peers while expressing their own individuality through the clothes and hairstyles that match the music's image. Think of the different images associated with Oasis, The Spice Girls and Prodigy.

Marketing and promotion

The 1990s saw the meteoric rise in the popularity of manufactured bands – that is, bands that are customised and marketed to appeal to mass audiences. This concept was nothing new, The Monkees set the trend in the 1960s, which was continued later with outstanding success by Take That and The Spice Girls.

Mass success depends on a number of factors: the tastes of the pop industry's giants, the approval of those who determine prestige and credibility, such as DJs and music journalists, and the power of '**A 'n' R**' people and **strike force** promoters, who push the artists into the limelight and ensure that they feature on radio **playlists**.

Of course, every band that produces pop music does not automatically become successful and, even in an industry that is driven by profit, money does not always mean success. In fact, the trend of manufacturing bands has created more failures than fantasies – do you remember Upside Down or Hepburn?

Away from the mainstream

There will always be some people who do not want to conform to the images associated with chart fodder. Musical **genres** such as speed garage, thrash metal and drum 'n' bass are created by urban subcultures rather than record companies and offer an alternative to mainstream music. These artistes are generally signed to independent record companies, such as Twisted Nerve, that rely more on reputation, word-of-mouth and the music press to promote their record sales. Their lack of mass promotion is seen by fans as a sign that their music has more value and integrity because it is not driven only by profit.

> Try applying the techniques listed on pages 16–17 for working out how you feel about a piece of classical music to one of your favourite pop songs. Do the same methods work with a different style of music? Does listening to pop music involve the same type of experiences as listening to classical music?

Marketing and promotion

The pop industry works closely with the tabloid press, providing the public with information, both true and false, about their favourite pop stars. As well as high-profile, front page stories about what is happening in the world of pop, there are specialised pop pages, which thrive on celebrity gossip. These stories focus on the stars' private lives and are often exaggerated, by their sources and the newspapers, for maximum impact. Pop videos provide exposure for bands and increase their visibility. They are shown on a large number of programmes, from the news to those directed at a youth market, and there are also entire channels devoted to them, such as MTV. They can be produced cheaply or on ever-escalating budgets, and it is not unusual for the notoriety of the video to enhance the popularity of a band.

A 'n' R – stands for Artists and Repertoire. People in the A 'n' R department are responsible for finding, developing and looking after bands, as well as managing image, sound, press outings and publicity.

GURU TIP
Music papers, such as NME, will provide the latest news and reviews, while the radio (especially Radio 1) will keep you up-to-date with information on pop artists and the latest musical trends.

Culture, morality, arts and humanities

The theatre

GURU WEBSITE

There's a lot of talk about funding theatres. Check out what the AS Guru™ website has to say about this on:

www.bbc.co.uk/asguru

Decide whether or not you think theatre should be as easily accessible as the cinema.

What comes to mind when you think about the theatre? Are its associations mainly positive or negative? Whatever your views, note them down because they could be of use in your AS General Studies exam. Questions about culture and the arts often ask how you view high and low culture, and what you can gain from the experience. Since theatre is generally considered to be a product of high culture, a knowledge of its strengths and limitations will help you develop your own point of view.

Compared to cinema, the theatre has obvious physical limitations. However, it has a wealth of experiences that other media cannot provide. These include:

- a direct relationship between the actors and the audience that is enhanced by the intimate setting of a theatre, especially if it is '**in the round**'
- an almost tangible creation of character relationships and emotions before you
- the atmosphere that can be created by the actors, and the lighting and the setting in a theatre, which involves you as you become part of the performance, rather than just a **passive consumer** of it
- a suspension of disbelief because the action can evoke extraordinarily powerful images that put across a meaning without being literal
- the fact that every performance is a one-off that can be different and spontaneous every night because it is live
- fresh interpretations that different directors and actors can give to old material.

This is the theory – but do you agree? Have you ever found that watching a play offers you this experience, or do you think that the cinema offers more? Rehearse your arguments with reference to your own example of **drama** and cinema-going experiences.

The theatre, society and politics

An examination question may ask you about the quality of the theatrical experience, and about what relevance theatre has in society. You will need to be able to show some knowledge of the history of the theatre and mention some prominent playwrights in order to add credibility to your answer. Here is some initial information as a starting point.

- Ever since theatre evolved as a popular pastime, it has been the platform upon which playwrights and actors could reflect upon political and social trends. The script was able to document the events of an era or express new or revolutionary ideas to a captive audience. For example, the **Medieval Mystery, Miracle and Morality plays** (600–1500) became popular theatre because they carried increasingly critical messages about how corrupt the ruling classes were.
- Some plays have been so controversial that rulers were outraged, theatres shut down as a result and actors executed because of their influence. In England, Oliver Cromwell (1599–1658) and the Puritans closed the theatres because of their power to inspire social discontent, and they were not re-opened until the restoration of King Charles II.
- You will probably be aware that many of the playwrights you came across when doing your GCSEs, from William Shakespeare to Willie Russell, have attempted to explain or challenge the ideas of the times in which they lived – you could use their work to illustrate your points. For example, *A Doll's House*, a play by Henrik Ibsen (1828–1906), attempted to change his society's prevalent attitude that women were the slaves of their husbands.

Likewise, JB Priestley (1894–1984) was a passionate social commentator and, in his play, *An Inspector Calls*, he successfully criticised the middle classes, which would have made up the majority of his audience, for their selfishness and greed. His motives were a belief in socialism and his desire not only to show what the industrial world had become, but also to make it a better place for the poorer classes. One character says:

'We are members of one body. We are responsible for each other. And I will tell you that the time will soon come when, if men will not learn that lesson, then they will be taught it in fire and blood and anguish.'

It is clear that, historically, the immediacy and direct access to a mass audience of the theatre, made it a powerful vehicle for playwrights who had a social conscience.

The audience as theatre

More recently, in the 1950s and 60s, Brazilian director, Augusto Boal, devised what he called 'Theatre of the Oppressed', or 'Forum Theatre', which has since become a theatrical tradition. Boal's idea was to begin a play and then stop the action at crucial points to ask the audience what they thought should happen next. He challenged the audience to think about the issues and confronted them with situations from which they could learn and question social norms.

Tragedy and comedy

Augusto Boal once said: 'While some people make theatre, we are all theatre.' What do you think he meant? Do you think that he is correct?

Although **tragedy** deals with uncontrollable and often terrible events, it entertains an audience. You may have studied a Shakespearean tragedy, such as *Hamlet* or *Romeo and Juliet*, which provide exciting and moving drama. They deal with momentous occasions that equate to experiences that most people will have, in some form, in their lives.

Issues, such as love, death and difficult dilemmas, are presented, enabling the audience to recognise elements of their own problems on stage. This forces the audience to reflect upon their own feelings and preoccupations about their lives. Tragedy can, therefore, provide an emotional release, which allows them to enjoy watching someone else's pain.

Comedy can have a similar effect. Laughter is a good way of releasing tension and you can laugh at the situations comedy provides because they deal with less serious issues than tragedy. It may seem perverse to find other people's misfortunes funny, but the amusement may be based on relief that the situations are not happening to you personally. **Dramatic irony** is commonly used in comedy, where the audience is privy to information that the characters are not.

Satire often provides the audience with social and political comment and draws heavily on topical issues and situations in the real world. This is exaggerated and distorted to create humorous situations. An audience which understands the topical links in the play will appreciate the humour. This type of humour often aims to expose the wrongdoings or actions of powerful figures (such as Mr Birling in *An Inspector Calls*) and a sympathetic audience can enjoy the imagined embarrassment of the exposure of these characters.

Culture, morality, arts and humanities

Cinema

Like the theatre, the cinema can be used in General Studies to discuss the differences between mass and minority tastes. You are likely to be more familiar with the cinema than the theatre, so you should be able to use this experience to your advantage.

Mainstream cinema is often regarded as a product of low culture, as it appeals to a mass audience. It can be understood by a wide range of people and could be said rarely to challenge your intellect. It is often accused of:

- influencing poor social behaviour, especially in the young
- reflecting a decline in moral standards
- 'dumbing down' important issues.

Do you agree or disagree with any of these accusations, and can you back up your arguments by referring to films that you have seen or reviews or research that you have read? Look out for film reviews and the broadsheet newspaper media supplements because these are an excellent source of information and comment about the film industry. You should also try to relate the points made in this section to films you have watched recently or know well.

Why do you go to the cinema?

You probably go to the cinema primarily to be entertained, especially if you choose to see a **mainstream film**. You would probably also say that it is better to watch a film at the cinema than on TV because of the advantages that the cinematic experience can provide.

The cinema's advantages:
- it offers the ultimate escapism
- it allows you to suspend disbelief in a darkened auditorium for a few hours
- it permits momentary distraction from the screen, yet you can immediately become re-absorbed in the film without any impairment to your enjoyment
- it controls your emotions, allowing you to become completely involved in non-stop action
- its huge images flash before you while sound is pumped at you from all sides, keeping you involved
- you can return to your own reality when you leave the cinema.

The disadvantages of watching a film on TV:
- having the remote control at your fingertips means that you control the film rather than the film controlling you, and this impairs involvement
- allowing the outside world to encroach (for example, if the phone rings) somehow lessens the magic of a film
- special effects do not seem so spectacular on a small screen
- you cannot enjoy the experience of sharing emotions with a mass of other people and so miss out on something that can enhance the atmosphere and tension
- going to the cinema is a social event, whereas watching TV is not.

GURU TIP

If you go to the cinema or watch a video in order to use the information about the film in a General Studies assignment, be sure to write up your findings as soon as you can so that your opinions are as clear as possible.

What happens when you watch a film?

There are many different theories that try to explain what effects the medium of cinema has on a mass audience. This section discusses two models that will help you develop your own point of view about this.

- The **hypodermic model:** this suggests that when you watch a film, meanings are 'injected' in to your mind as if by a powerful syringe, so that you are drugged or duped by the values and ideologies that the film portrays. For example, most mainstream films are American and therefore promote American values and ideologies to the rest of the world, which may explain why America influences British youth culture so much. Tied in with this model is the idea that audiences can be influenced to commit violent acts after watching violence in a film, and so films should be censored until they are fit for a mass audience. The film *Natural Born Killers* was eventually banned because of its portrayal of violence and concerns over what effects this would have on the public. Could this approach make film a scapegoat for society's ills? Film director Oliver Stone, speaking in June 1995, would say not. He commented:

  'It is the height of hypocrisy for Senator Dole (Republican Presidential candidate) who wants to repeal the assault weapons ban, to blame Hollywood for the violence in our society'.

- The **uses and gratifications model:** this suggests that when you watch a film you do so to fulfil your own needs. Instead of being duped, the theory goes, as an individual in a mass audience, you have your own power to understand or adapt the meanings that a film portrays as you choose. You could argue that when films use devices such as disjointed narratives – where different characters are used to develop two or more stories that eventually 'join up' – one of the most fulfilling experiences of watching a film can be working out the missing links and piecing together the narrative. If you have seen *The Sixth Sense*, for example, you will have experienced this effect. If you have not, can you think of a film that has kept you guessing?

Which model do you think is correct? Are you duped by the ideologies that films present? Do film directors attempt to dupe you? Do you adapt the meaning of a film to fit your ideas? Rehearse your arguments with reference to your favourite films.

The British Board of Film Classification (BBFC)

The BBFC certifies film and video using the following classifications:

- **U** universal – suitable for all
- **Uc** universal – particularly suitable for young children
- **PG** parental guidance – general viewing but some scenes may be unsuitable for young children
- **12** suitable only for persons of 12 years and over
- **15** suitable only for persons of 15 years and over
- **18** suitable only for persons of 18 years and over.

BBFC examiners watch each film about to go on general release and decide on what the public should (and shouldn't) see. The censorship that the BBFC can operate is not necessarily based on legal requirements but on what the examiners think may or may not offend audiences. Staff at the BBFC must agree not to discuss their decisions outside the workplace. This is possible because the BBFC is a private company funded by the film industry, which was set up to prevent government control over what is released and what people watch on the big screen.

GURU TIP
It doesn't matter where you stand on the debate about how a film's audience reacts. In an AS General Studies exam it is important that you back up what you say with evidence and provide the examiner with a balanced and thoughtful argument.

Stuart Hall, a media researcher, suggested that audiences have particular responses when watching films:

dominant – go along with the messages and bias of the text as reasonable

oppositional – disagree outright with the opinions

middle ground – agree with the text so far but modify it with personal experiences.

GURU WEBSITE
Visit the AS Guru™ website at www.bbc.co.uk/asguru for an interview with Anthony Minghella, the director of *The Talented Mr Ripley*.

Culture, morality, arts and humanities

Literature

Here are some popular classics that have been made into films:

- **Lord of the Flies**
  – William Golding

- **A Kestrel for a Knave (Kes)**
  – Barry Hines

- **Of Mice and Men**
  – John Steinbeck

- **Oliver Twist (Oliver!)**
  – Charles Dickens

- many plays by William Shakespeare.

KEY SKILLS

To achieve Key Skill C3.3, write a student leaflet defending the use of film versions of texts in school. Write a speech for teachers arguing the other side of the debate. Use language that is relevant for your audiences and purpose.

KEY SKILLS C3.3

One of the ideas that has been highlighted in this section has been the conflict between high culture and popular culture. This idea is equally relevant to the subject of literature in General Studies. You may be asked:

- whether works considered to be 'classics' by writers such as Dickens, Austen and Shakespeare should be popularised by making them into films
- what can be gained or lost in a film adaptation of a novel or a play
- how the experience of watching a film adaptation is different from the experience of reading the original novel or play.

Recently, there has been a succession of Hollywood versions of 'classics', for example Edith Wharton's *The House of Mirth*, Graham Greene's *The End of the Affair*, John Irving's *The Cider House Rules* and Jane Austen's *Mansfield Park*.

As it is highly probable that you will have watched a film adaptation of a 'classic' novel or play through studying English Literature at GCSE, you should be able to develop your own viewpoint with conviction. Remember, you do not have to agree totally with one point of view over another; try to balance your argument with points for and points against, and then sum up with your own personal conclusion. Here are two viewpoints that will help you to shape your responses.

> 'Hollywood appears to be concentrating its efforts on making films for a young audience with a disposable income. The tendency is away from script and content and towards a technological veneer . . .'
>
> Jill Nelmes (ed), *An Introduction to Film Studies*
>
> 'Expertly observed and performed adaptation of Edith Wharton's novel, *The House of Mirth* . . . Terence Davies' ravishing period drama exceeds all expectations.'
>
> Film review, The Guide in *The Guardian*, 28.10.00

In support of films of classic texts

- They are a way of introducing classic works in popular form to a greater number of people.
- They could whet the appetite and encourage a new interest in literature (and the arts in general), which is considered to be more classical.
- People might be encouraged to read the real thing.
- The themes of classical works are still retained in films and could therefore still confront and challenge people.
- Objections to film adaptations could be dismissed as academic snobbery.
- You could argue that some films are better than books as they can appeal more immediately to all of your senses, creating the ultimate aesthetic experience.
- Some classics, such as the novels of Dickens, were written in instalments and so translate successfully to TV adaptations.
- Some writers have consciously written novels with the stage or cinema in mind, such as John Steinbeck in *Of Mice and Men*; others have used film techniques in the writing of their novels so that the film can enhance the meaning of the story, such as John Fowles in *The French Lieutenant's Woman*.
- Some stories are larger than life and a film version can envelop you emotionally in a way only a spectacular cinema film version can only do. Film can often evoke atmospheres and settings more effectively than a book.

Against films of classic texts

- Film adaptations reflect yet more 'dumbing down' of works that should expand the imagination.
- Appreciation of the author's use of rich vocabulary, **imagery** and grammar is easily lost, so written texts should not be made easier by reducing them to visual images and simple dialogue.
- Subtle **nuances** of meaning are lost as characters are often simplified or stereotyped to ease understanding, so the film cannot be as fulfilling as the book.
- Some works of literature have become 'classics' because they have proved to be popular through the ages, so why would they need popularising any further?
- A film director's, or someone else's, interpretation of a work can ruin your own imaginative perceptions of it. You ought to be able to consider and reflect upon a text using your own imagination.
- You cannot replicate the rich experience of reading a novel as you watch a film. Novels develop your thoughts and the characters and context are created together. Writers interact with readers – it is a two-way process. On the other hand, a film is a one-way process – you have to see things from the director's point of view, who will create the meanings for you.

Developing your own point of view

As you formulate your answers, try to use as many examples of classic works as possible. Generally speaking, any work that you have studied for an exam or done for coursework in English Literature can be considered a classic. Think what value it contributed to your course of study:

- did the film or play not live up to the book because the pictures you developed in your mind about the characters and settings were not as you had imagined?
- did it enhance your enjoyment because it brought the story alive?
- did it make issues clearer and help you picture things you hadn't seen before?
- did it enhance your understanding or help you see things in another way?
- was it the only opportunity that you got to see, for example, a Shakespeare play performed because the production was touring as you studied?

Your answer will be stronger if you can use your own experiences and points of view, rather than just attack the question hypothetically. If you passed your GCSE Literature examination, then a General Studies literature question is one that you should be able to answer convincingly.

Certain authors have exposed their points of view about what happens when people read. These alternative points of view can make an interesting and valuable input to exam essays. If you have access to the Internet, try using a search engine (such as www.google.com) to find out about the following people:

- Henry James
- Virginia Woolf
- Maurice Sendak

These people all have strong ideas about the special relationship that can exist between reader and writer, who share in the creation of an imagined world. Literature can, therefore, be seen to feed the imagination, an important human function, whereas film interpretation could be said to do the imagining for you.

Have you seen Baz Luhrman's version of *Romeo & Juliet*, Channel 4's *Macbeth on the Estate* or Kenneth Branagh's version of *Love's Labour's Lost*? They are good examples of original ways of reinterpreting traditional Shakespeare plays.

GURU TIP
Try taking a scene from a book that you know well and compare it with the same scene as portrayed in a film. For example, the fight scene between Lennie and Curly in *Of Mice and Men*. Compare the effectiveness of both and practise an answer based on this.

Have you seen any films that are rewritten versions of classics, such as *West Side Story* (*Romeo and Juliet*); *Ten Things I Hate about You* (*The Taming of the Shrew*); or *Clueless* (*Emma*). Do you think these adaptations are valuable?

Culture, morality, arts and humanities

Modern art

Modern art is a tricky subject to tackle because people generally find it intimidating. You can probably tell whether a traditional painting has **aesthetic** value, but what about a dead lamb frolicking in formaldehyde – is that art? Modern art, therefore, challenges ideas about what art is and always generates heated debate, along the lines of other 'popular versus high culture' arguments. Consequently, it is a useful topic on which to formulate your ideas at AS level.

What is art?

Art is a general term that refers to a range of art forms including:
- painting and drawing
- sculpture
- architecture
- photography
- crafts such as metalwork and pottery, etc.

Most people tend to think of painting when they think of art. This is because it has been one of the most dominant art forms in our culture for the past few centuries. Painting is generally considered to be the art form most capable of producing perfect visual images, and certain pictures are often referred to as 'fine art' to set them apart from other arts that are seen as being less worthy in comparison.

Although painting still has immense popularity as an art form, it seems that attitudes towards this artistic medium are changing. Out of all of the art forms nominated for the 1999 Turner Prize, not one of them was a painting. Instead, there was Tracey Emin's *My Bed* (an unmade bed) and Steve McQueen's film piece, *Deadpan*, which finally won.

Are modern tastes changing?

It may not be accurate to say that modern tastes towards art are changing wholesale, but there is certainly more interest in modern art than ever before. Why is this? Certainly, the following have helped:
- the opening of the Tate Modern, a gallery dedicated to modern art
- high profile awards like the Tate-sponsored Turner Prize
- equally high-profile exhibitions, such as *Sensation* held at the Royal Academy of Arts in 1999, showcasing what were supposed to be the most sensational items of modern art in the world
- media hype covering the above events and general sensationalising of modern art
- modern art's affiliation with popular culture that started with Andy Warhol's association with '60s band The Velvet Underground and has been maintained, for example, by Damien Hirst's collaborations with Blur.

What is the subject of modern art?

Like more traditional art, modern art is made up of old images with new interpretations. One of the current trends is exhibits (referred to as 'installations') that are made up of everyday items. Unlike a traditional painting, the meaning isn't generally concentrated on a single object, but on an array of items arranged to construct other meanings, such as:
- the artist's clothing and personal items, telling you something of their past
- ordinary items, such as worn mattresses, melons, buckets and cucumbers representing ideas about sexuality
- dead and sliced-up animals, illustrating death.

> Art is any form of creative work that has significance. It can exercise human skill, both physically and mentally, in the artist and the viewer.

GURU TIP
Look up the Tate Modern and other gallery websites, and read listings pages in weekend broadsheet newspapers to see where the nearest modern art exhibition is in your area. Visit it, so that you can exemplify your General Studies answers and gain extra marks.

You could say that by using such mundane and ordinary subjects, modern art gives us a more realistic representation of contemporary culture. You could also say that modern art attempts to express the issues of the times in a new way, befitting the 21st Century. Or you could dismiss modern art altogether as an elaborate con. Whatever you think, you will provoke a debate.

The shock factor

Modern art is also notorious for its shock factor. It seems a prerequisite of recent modern art that you should be shocked by it. However, you may think that, today, a head filled with human blood, children's hand paintings of Myra Hindley's face and sawn-up dead cows in formaldehyde at the *Sensation* exhibition may not be all that shocking in theory, but did manage to shock because:

- they were real and the reality of these installations made them more shocking than paintings
- they were sights you don't see every day which made them intriguing
- the media said that they were shocking
- people like to be shocked.

Therefore, shock could also be considered a contributory factor that helps to explain modern art's growing popularity.

What does it all mean?

Does it mean anything at all? One argument in favour of modern art suggests that the meanings are not deeply ingrained and, like other media of popular culture, anyone can understand it, even if they don't like it. Surely, appreciating art should give pleasure and if you get pleasure from looking at modern art, or if it makes you think, then it does have value, whether you think modern artists are geniuses or charlatans.

Conversely, you may want to argue about the authenticity of the work of modern artists. You could probably accurately recreate some modern art yourself because it is about interpreting concepts, rather than using traditional artistic talents. It can therefore appear less skilful than more traditional art forms, but does that mean that it has less worth than more traditional art?

Tracey Emin (b. 1963) an artist who uses sometimes shocking, intimate details of her own life as the subject matter of her artwork. One of her most famous works is her Turner Prize shortlisted exhibit *My Bed*.

Damien Hirst (b. 1965) an artist whose work deals with the themes of birth, life, love and death. A Turner Prize winner, his most notorious pieces involve dead animals. He is also well known for making pop videos, and is mostly associated with Blur.

Andy Warhol (d 1987) an artist and experimental filmmaker, who was at the centre of the Pop Art movement of the 1960s. Some of his most famous work took famous people and images of death as its subjects.

GURU TIP
Why not try researching other art movements? Use the following suggestions as a starting point, or key words to type into an Internet search engine.

Cubism: Braque, Duchamp and Picasso.

Surrealism: Dali, Miro and Magritte.

Pop art: Lichtenstein, Rauschenberg and Warhol.

Culture, morality, arts and humanities

GURU TIP
You could argue in support of, or in opposition to modern art equally successfully, but you will be more convincing if your argument is based on your own point of view and balanced against other people's, so make sure you have one!

Advertising

What is advertising?

Adverts contain messages from manufacturers, which have been created by advertising agencies, whose business it is to make large numbers of potential customers aware of a product or service. Advertising also generates a great deal of revenue for advertising agencies, television channels, magazines and any other medium that carries them, as well as the company that has made the product or offers the service, and it is therefore an incredibly lucrative business.

How many adverts have you seen or heard today?

It would not be an exaggeration to estimate that everyone has been subjected to some form of advertising today, either consciously or subconsciously. It may have been on a billboard, on the radio or television, in a magazine, in a newspaper or on the side of a bus. It may have been for a luxury product or service, for public information, or in support of a charity. You will not have been subjected to this advertising by mistake. It will have been played, positioned or planned to be consumed by the right person, in the right context, at the right time. The aim of advertising, therefore, is to make sure that the subject of the advertisement is put right in front of the target audience.

How are target audiences located?

Advertisers use market research to build up profiles of particular class-, age-, occupation- and gender-related groups, whose habits can be recognised, which makes the task of promoting products and targetting audiences more accurate. Market research is also used to find out what potential audiences are thinking and feeling and to discover new styles and trends. Advertisers can then use this information to create lifestyle images in their adverts that will appeal to their target audiences and encourage them to buy into the promise of this lifestyle by purchasing the product or service. You can all probably remember buying a product because of the image the advertisers sold you. So, advertisers claim to use society itself, to dictate the content of their adverts.

GURU TIP

When you are looking at adverts, form a viewpoint and gather evidence to support or reject the claim that adverts reflect trends in society.

How advertising reflects trends in society

'Advertising holds a mirror up to the way society is'.
Rita Clifton, Interbrand Group

Rita Clifton is the CEO of Interbrand Group, an international company and product branding consultancy.

It is clear how certain products in different decades have promoted the trends that reflected popular thinking. The 1980s were dominated by images of affluent, high-consuming 'yuppies'. Adverts for cars during this time were concerned more with status, style and success than with the actual features of the product. The 1990s offered more socially and environmentally sensitive images, such as the male who appeared in the *Fairy Liquid* campaign, washing dishes. In 2000, the changing roles of men and women and the changing nature of society in general seem to have set the trend. Adverts for household products and food, such as the *Bisto* family, used to promote traditional family values, whereas a recent *Ikea* advert encouraged consumers to celebrate a divorce by buying new furniture. Can you think of any current adverts that promote modern trends in society?

Advertising and ideology

Many academic theorists have looked much deeper into the impact advertising has on society. Instead of society dictating the content of adverts, they believe that the images we see in adverts reinforce conservative, dominant ideology (the dominant set of ideas and values within a society). This idea suggests that adverts instil in us ideals about how we should be living our life and what we should think about certain issues. Advertising agencies have also been accused of sustaining stereotypical images that we have of certain sectors of society through their portrayal in adverts, and of creating dissatisfaction with life, especially among young people. Do you think that adverts are really so powerful, that they have effects beyond stimulating the need to buy?

It could be argued that the powerful imagery used in adverts will inevitably convey certain cultural values. For example, women are still predominantly featured in adverts about eating chocolate, being in supermarkets or in a domestic situation, and men are likewise seen in the office, the executive car or drinking beer.

> 'It (advertising) doesn't lead trends; it doesn't create needs where they currently don't exist. And I guess if your problem is with society as it is, advertising will always offend.'
>
> Rita Clifton, Interbrand Group

Therefore, the way that these values have been portrayed to the consumer could be seen as an important factor in helping to sustain the dominant ideology which characterises society at certain points in time. But do these values reflect the views of the consumer? Are we subliminally brainwashed into believing in the mythical world of the advertiser, or are we more sophisticated at understanding media images than ever before? What do you, as consumers, think?

Some academics and people who produce adverts do not believe that advertising reinforces the dominant conservative ideology. They claim that the only aim of an advert is to sell something. How far do you think the advertising agencies are willing to go, in terms of manipulating your subconscious?

Do you agree with this statement?

When analysing the impact of adverts on society, you need to decide whether the images that you see have been manipulated to achieve a certain effect, and whether their ultimate effect was intended to reflect the status quo or not. For example, has the woman on the Renault Clio advert been chosen because she is sophisticated and sexually provocative and can seduce potential buyers, or has she been chosen to represent the current status and values attributed to women in today's society?

You could also ask yourself what other factors came into play when you made your last purchase. Did you buy the product because:

- you'd used it before and liked it?
- because a friend had recommended it to you?
- because you had read reviews about it?
- because the price was right?

Perhaps if we didn't have other sources of information at our disposal, advertising would influence us much more. What do you think?

GURU TIP
Think about the adverts that you have come across today and the ways you are subjected to advertising.

Culture, morality, arts and humanities

GURU WEBSITE
Visit the *Selling Point* section on the AS Guru™ General Studies website at:

www.bbc.bo.uk/asguru

Television news

One of the most important resources for your General Studies AS course is the television news.

You will need to watch it for two reasons:
- to keep up with current affairs
- to be aware of the phenomenon of TV news itself.

In your examination, you will be asked about current affairs and you could be asked about the ways in which TV news influences public opinion; its disadvantages and advantages in comparison to other news media; whether it is biased, or how it treats issues of national and international importance.

If you asked your peers whether they watched the news, they would probably say no. However unappealing you may find it, it is very influential and determines the scheduling of virtually all other programmes. It is broadcast at regular intervals during the day with the main news bulletins scheduled in the evenings both to fit in with audience lifestyle and as a convenient time to report on the day's stories.

> According to research done by Channel 5 prior to launching its prize-winning news programme, less than 16% of 16–24 year olds watch any news.

Popularity of television news

People have now become more dependent on the television as their main source of news than any other medium because:
- it simplifies complicated issues
- it tells you about things in a narrative form with pictures to illustrate
- it can be consumed more effortlessly than a newspaper or a radio report
- it has become the most easily accessible source of knowledge and understanding about the world.

All the reasons, listed above, mean that television news is a powerful phenomenon. You could say that reading a selection of broadsheet newspapers will give you a more detailed understanding of an issue, but TV news is particularly influential because it can reach a mass audience and people tend to trust it because it is on the television. Do you think they are right to do so? After all, the television news is a media product and, like any other product, it is created to influence you in certain ways.

> **Major national bulletins**
>
> *BBC News*, 6 pm and 10 pm (BBC 1)
>
> *Newsnight*, 10.30 pm (BBC 2)
>
> *ITV News*, 6.30 pm and 10 pm (ITV)
>
> *Channel 4 News*, 7 pm (Channel 4)
>
> *5 News*, 6 pm (Channel 5)

How is the news chosen?

Information cascades into newsrooms from an array of sources, including international news agencies, such as Reuters, local news agencies, the government, the courts and industry representatives. It is the responsibility of the board of editors to decide what information is newsworthy and what the public must know about. Of the millions of events that happen every day, only a few reach our screens. One theory that attempts to explain this is **news values**. A story will have news value if:
- it has good visuals – TV depends on visual images and people will be more likely to believe an event if they see it
- it is a new story or an 'exclusive' that has happened that day – 'old' stories are yesterday's news
- it contains bad news because negative events are easier to turn into dramatic narratives than good news, as are conflicts and scandals
- it has happened on a large scale and affected a lot of people
- it involves famous people
- it is unpredictable and unusual
- it is anticipated, such as a sporting event
- it has happened in this country.

Scheduling content

As well as using news values, news stories need to have a specific running order to ensure they are 'audience friendly'. Main bulletins generally contain a mix of story types. The running order is typically:

- **hard news** (more serious) items run at the start of the programme
- as the programme progresses, items become 'softer'
- sport and weather follow
- the broadcast ends with the heart-warming item designed to reassure you that life is not all that bad.

This balance of content is as important in determining which stories are used as news values. News programmes are as much a part of the battle for viewing figures as any other programme on television.

Money

Another factor that determines news content is money. Television news is an expensive business so, in order to ensure good returns, news agencies need to send their crews to profitable stories (ones that will gain them a large audience). For example, if there is a conflict in a small country, it is likely to go unnoticed unless a major power becomes involved. Conversely, it ensures that issues from Washington, the football Premiership and the entertainment industries will feature regularly.

Neutrality

There are rules governing neutrality in news bulletins to ensure that both sides of the argument are presented equally and fairly, however, bias can be introduced into the programme in other ways:

- camera positioning – in a riot scene, the pictures maybe taken from the viewpoint of the rioters' frontline or the frontline of the police force
- the interviewing of guests in a hard or soft style
- choice of eye-witness – either supportive of, or against, the subject
- words used to describe an event or organisation. For example, are participants involved in an uprising referred to as 'freedom fighters' or 'terrorists'?

Impartiality is also required in news bulletins, which means that any controversial issue must have both sides of the argument presented, and what is fact and what is opinion must be made clear.

Every time you watch the news, be aware of all of the factors that affect the way an issue is reported. Think hard about what you are being shown. Try to decide whether you are getting a biased viewpoint, and question the way events have been chosen, ordered, manipulated and portrayed to affect your understanding of the world.

Scheduling content

Content on a news programme is presented in a certain way so that you can easily digest information that would otherwise be dull and factual. The use of film or video inserts, **vox pops** and interviews, location shooting, live action and in-shot narrators enable us to draw parallels between the news and variety or chat shows. Along with the central star personality (the newsreader) who holds it all together and concludes the show comfortably, you can see that the news is packaged like many other programmes to be as attractive and entertaining as possible.

KEY SKILLS

Ask your group to analyse the news values in the content schedules of different television news programmes, over a week. Ask them to email their results to you and use spreadsheets, pie and bar charts to present your results.

GURU TIP

Analyse the structure of a news bulletin. Ask yourself the following questions:

- What is the lead story and why does it have priority?
- What is the ratio of 'hard' news to 'soft' stories. How are they distributed in the programme?
- What news value does each story carry? Are the values the same on other programmes?

GURU TIP

Watch carefully when an issue you feel strongly about is reported. Is the coverage fair and thorough or biased and lacking in detail? Will this coverage influence people's opinions of the issue? What effect could this have?

Culture, morality, arts and humanities

Practice questions

Try the following essay questions which encourage you to look at issues in a certain way and are the kind that you are likely to get on an exam paper.

1 To what extent does artistic talent contribute to success in the pop industry?

2 Do we need morals in the 21st Century?

3 Discuss whether you think religion does more harm than good.

4 Will advertising always be offensive to someone?

5 How far do you agree that television news programmes depend on negative news values to sustain viewing figures?

6 What function does modern art have?

7 Should art and music be compulsory at GCSE and what could students gain from this?

8 Write about a work of art (e.g. play, painting, musical composition), giving reasons why you liked or disliked it.

Key points

When answering General Studies questions on this domain, you should:

- ALWAYS plan your answer to give it flow and structure: underline key words in the question; write down all the facts and opinions you know about the subject; arrange these points to construct your argument. Planned responses always score more highly than unplanned ones;

- ALWAYS choose questions which you know something about, bearing in mind your own breadth of knowledge, strengths and weaknesses; be familiar with the material you are dealing with: for example do not condemn the work of Mozart if you have only heard it once;

- ALWAYS be objective: for example, if you don't enjoy the theatre do not judge it by your personal standards. As in all subjects, always appreciate the good things in what you are examining; being negative or dismissive is not as effective;

- ALWAYS avoid irrelevancies – don't regurgitate a response you've written previously on a subject if it is not quite the same question; make every sentence count!

- ALWAYS check over your response to ensure that what you have written makes sense, is expressed as clearly as possible and your spelling, punctuation and grammar are accurate.

Maths

In this section you will be learning about:

☞ number, shape and space

☞ functions and graphs

☞ algebra

☞ statistics and probability

☞ algorithms and networks.

The importance of maths is demonstrated to us each and every day. Even those AS level candidates who will not be using specific aspects of maths in their future careers will need to be able to use the basic skills in the adult world – comparing mortgage rates from various sources, reading information given in tables when booking holidays, understanding statistics given in newspapers or calculating areas when covering floors in the house. All these can be done for you by the banks, the travel agent and the carpet retailer, but you need to be sure that you are getting the best deal and you would be surprised (and concerned) by the mistakes professionals can make.

Mathematical skills are used in a wide range of contexts, for example consider a journey along a British motorway. The speed limit at the approach to the motorway junction or roundabout will have been calculated to guarantee the car will negotiate the curve of the bend safely. The motorway bridges will have been designed by engineers using geometry and trigonometry. You might pass through a police speed check – these use numerical calculations (the lines on the road are set so that timing a car between them can be easily translated into an average speed over that piece of road). If you are unlucky and have to sit in a traffic jam caused by roadworks to add an extra lane or redesign a section of the motorway, remember the systems analyst who collected the data used to propose the plans for the developments.

Maths is required by a wide range of students, not only those taking the subject at AS level. Other subjects are supported by certain mathematical concepts or techniques and you will be able to adapt the basic skills you learn here to your particular needs in the future. However, for the moment, your priority must be to understand the basic concepts and master the procedures involved to make sure you achieve the highest mark you can on the mathematics section of your AS General Studies paper.

Number, shape and space

Number has been vital since the earliest times – time was measured by the angles of the sun and stars, farmers measured their land and traders calculated weight and volume. As it was not always possible to solve problems with whole numbers, decimals and fractions were used.

Fractions

Although today calculators, computers and metric measurements mean that fractions are used less frequently, it is still important to know how to use them.

To simplify fractions, you find the common factor on the **numerators** and **denominators** (top and bottom numbers). Divide them by the common factor and simplify it.

For example: $\frac{24}{48} = \frac{1}{2}$ (÷ 24)

Adding and subtracting

The denominators must be the same.

EXAMPLE $\frac{2}{3} + \frac{3}{4}$

SOLUTION You need a number that both 3 and 4 will divide into. The smallest number that does this, is 12, so change both fractions into twelfths:

$$\frac{2}{3} = \frac{8}{12} \Rightarrow \frac{3}{4} = \frac{9}{12} \Rightarrow \frac{8}{12} + \frac{9}{12} = \frac{17}{12} = 1\frac{5}{12}$$

Multiplying

EXAMPLE $\frac{1}{3} \times 1\frac{3}{4}$

SOLUTION First change any **mixed number** into an **improper fraction**.

$$\frac{1}{3} \times 1\frac{3}{4} = \frac{1}{3} \times \frac{7}{4} = \frac{7}{12}$$ ← This is the simplest form of this fraction.

Then multiply the numerators and the denominators.

Dividing

EXAMPLE $2\frac{1}{3} \div \frac{1}{4}$

SOLUTION First change any mixed number into an improper fraction.

$$2\frac{2}{3} \div \frac{1}{4} = \frac{8}{3} \div \frac{1}{4} = \frac{8}{3} \times \frac{4}{1} = \frac{32}{3} = 10\frac{2}{3}$$ ← You can cancel to a mixed number

Then turn the fraction you are dividing by upside down and multiply.

Using a scientific calculator

Calculators vary, but most have an key.

> Remember, there is a specific order, in which you have to perform sums with fractions: × or ÷ before + or −
>
> A good way to memorise this is **BOMDAS**:
>
> **B**rackets **O**f **M**ultiply **D**ivide **A**dd **S**ubtract

EXAMPLE Work out $\frac{18.41 + 2.9}{12.6 - 1.5}$

SOLUTION a) rough answer: 22 ÷ 11 = 2

b) exact answer (using brackets to help)

$$\frac{18.41 + 2.9}{12.6 - 1.5} = (18.41 + 2.9) \div (12.6 - 1.5) = 1.9198198$$

GURU TIP

Estimate what the answer should be before you start and check your answer at the end of a calculation to make sure it seems sensible.

GURU TIP

Multiply a number by a fraction smaller than 1, and the answer will be less than the original number.

Divide a number by a fraction smaller than 1, and the answer will be bigger than the original number.

KEY SKILLS

If you conduct a survey, in any of your subjects, perform a statistical test, to validate the data (your tutor will help with this). Remember to show each stage of your calculation, even if you are using a calculator, in order to gain Key Skill N3.2.

Properties of numbers

These have fascinated researchers and mathematicians for centuries.

Factors are numbers that divide into other numbers exactly: 1, 2 and 5 are factors of 10 (remember to include 10 itself).

EXAMPLE   What are the factors of 18?   **S**OLUTION   1, 2, 3, 6, 9, 18

Multiples are the numbers that factors divide into: 12 is a multiple of 1, 2, 3, 4, 6 and 12 (again include 12 itself).

EXAMPLE   What are the first five multiples of 3?   **S**OLUTION   3, 6, 9, 12, 15

Prime numbers have exactly 2 factors.
Note: 1 is not a prime number and 2 is the only even prime number.

Powers

The term a^n (where a and n represent numbers) means a multiplied by itself n times. n is called the **power** (or **exponent** or **index**).

For example $8^3 = 8 \times 8 \times 8 = 512$

$$5 \times 5 \times 3 \times 3 \times 3 \times 3 = 5^2 \times 3^4$$

Note that $2^3 = 8$, so the cube root of 8 is 2 (this can be written as $\sqrt[3]{8} = 2$).

When **multiplying**, you add indices:

The general rules for zero and negative indices are:

$x^0 = 1$ for example $4^0 = 1$

or $x^{-5} = \frac{1}{x^5}$ for example $2^{-3} = \frac{1}{2^3} = \frac{1}{8}$

$4^2 \times 4^3 = 4^5$

When **dividing**, you subtract indices:

$7^9 \div 7^3 = 7^6$

Standard form

When dealing with either very large or very small numbers, it is inconvenient to write them out in full. It is easier to use **standard form** – a sort of maths shorthand.

For example, the speed of light is 300 000 km per second. Scientists will write this as 3×10^5 km per second.

EXAMPLE   Write 7 580 000 000 in standard form.   **S**OLUTION $= 7.58 \times 10^9$

Using a calculator for powers and standard form

Use y^x or x^y depending on your calculator.

EXAMPLE   Use your calculator to work out 2^8, which is '2 to the power of 8'.

SOLUTION   2 y^x 8 = 256 or 2 x^y 8 = 256

Don't confuse y^x and x^y with the | EE | and |EXP| key.

You use EE or EXP when you say 'times 10 to the power of ...'

EXAMPLE 2×10^8 means '2 times 10 to the power of 8'

SOLUTION   2 EXP 8 = 200 000 000

Percentages

Percentages are a way of writing fractions. Every percentage is a fraction with 100 as the denominator.

Some percentages are easy to calculate mentally. You know that:

$\frac{1}{2}$ = 50% $\frac{1}{4}$ = 25% $\frac{1}{10}$ = 10%

You can use these figures to help you find many other percentages.

EXAMPLE   At present, the VAT rate is 17.5%. Shannon buys a television that costs £270 + VAT. How much VAT does Shannon pay?

SOLUTION   Although this looks difficult to calculate, you can 'break up' the calculation.

10% of £270 = £27

5% of £270 = half of 10% = £13.50

2.5% of £270 = half of 5% = £6.75

10% + 5% + 2.5% = 17.5%

17.5% of £270 = £27 + £13.50 + £6.75 = £47.25

Percentages can easily be changed into decimals, which is a useful way to answer a variety of questions involving percentages.

$$\text{Percentage increase} = \frac{\text{actual increase}}{\text{original value}} \times \frac{100}{1}$$

$$\text{Percentage decrease} = \frac{\text{actual decrease}}{\text{original value}} \times \frac{100}{1}$$

$$\text{Percentage profit} = \frac{\text{actual profit}}{\text{cost price}} \times \frac{100}{1}$$

$$\text{Percentage loss} = \frac{\text{actual loss}}{\text{cost price}} \times \frac{100}{1}$$

EXAMPLE   A local newspaper sold 25 600 copies last week. If it sells 28 650 this week, by what percentage have sales increased?

SOLUTION   Actual increase: 28 650 − 25 600 = 3050

Percentage increase: $\frac{3050}{25\ 600} \times 100 = 11.9\%$

Metric and imperial units

The **metric** system has replaced the **imperial** system that was once used in the UK.

The metric units are:

1 kilometre = 1000 metres   1 litre = 1000 millilitres

1 metre = 1000 millimetres   1 kilogram = 1000 grams

1 metre = 100 centimetres

As imperial units are still used occasionally, it is important for you to know how to convert one unit into another.

1 inch = 2.54 centimetres   1 gallon = 4.55 litres

GURU WEBSITE

The AS Guru™ website has a section on working out percentages that you can try out. Visit it at www.bbc.co.uk/asguru to try the questions.

GURU TIP

Most packaging has a mass (in kilograms or grams) or capacity (in l, ml, cl). Look at packets to develop an idea of the size and mass of a variety of objects. It will give you a reference point when deciding whether the answers you have calculated are sensible.

1 mile = 1.61 kilometre   1 kilometre = 0.621 mile

1 pound = 0.454 kilogram   1 litre = 0.22 gallons

1 pint = 0.568 litre   1 kilogram = 2.2 pound

EXAMPLE Work out 3 pints in litres.

SOLUTION   1 pint = 0.568 litres

Therefore 3 pints = 0.568 × 3

= 1.70 litres (to 3 sf)

Sometimes you will be asked to give an answer to a number of 'significant figures'. This gives an approxiation to the number. The number 327, given to 2 significant figures would be 330 – as the figure 7 is greater than 5, it makes the 2 increase to 3.

Round up if the next figure ≥ 5   Round down if the next figure < 5

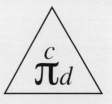

GURU TIP

Try memorising conversions using these rhymes:

'A metre is about three foot three, it is just over a yard you see!'

'Two point two pounds of jam is just about a kilogram.'

'A litre of water is a pint and three-quarters.'

Maths

Important formulae

You must learn these formulae, as they will not be provided in the exam.

Area of a triangle = $\frac{1}{2}$ base (b) × height (h)

(Base and height are perpendicular to each other.)

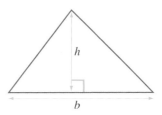

For a circle, the radius (r) = $\frac{1}{2}$ of diameter (d)

Area of a circle = $\pi \times r^2 = \pi r^2$

Circumference (c) of a circle = πd or $2\pi r$

Area of a parallelogram = base (b) × perpendicular height (h) (Perpendicular height is not one of the sides.) Remember: perpendicular means 'at right angles'.

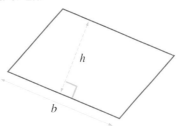

GURU TIP

For circle formulae, use this image of a table with a cat on top and a dog below:

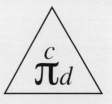

$$\frac{c}{\pi d}$$

Volume of a cuboid = length (l) × width (w) × height (h)

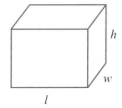

Volume of a prism = area of cross-section × length

(A prism is an object with a uniform cross-section.)

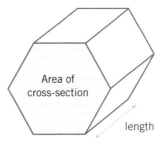

Area is measured in square units – you multiply 2 measurements.

Volume is measured in cubic units– you multiply 3 measurements.

Before reading this section, ask your General Studies Co-ordinator whether the topics explained here are on your syllabus.

> Basic angle facts:
> - angles at a point add up to 360°
> - angles on a straight line total 180°

Triangle angle facts

The angles of a triangle add up to 180°.

Equilateral triangles
- all angles are 60°
- 3 lines of symmetry (each line would cut the triangle into two right-angled triangles)

Isosceles triangles
- two equal sides and two equal angles
- 1 line of symmetry (it cuts the triangle into two right-angled triangles)

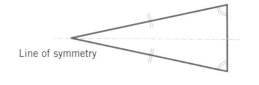

Line of symmetry

With a **scalene triangle** all three sides and all three angles are different.

> **GURU TIP**
> Corresponding angles: – you correspond with a Friend
>
> Alternate angles – learn your angles from A to Z.

Parallel line angle facts

Alternate angles are equal.

Corresponding angles are equal.

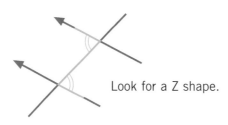

Look for a Z shape.

Look for an F shape (in this case, it's backwards: ꟻ).

Opposite angles are also equal.

Bearings

Bearings are used by ships, aircraft and mountaineers to guide them. They are used for direction where there are no roads.

> **GURU TIP**
> Make sure you know how to:
> - use alternate angles (z angles) with parallel lines pointing North
> - subtract from 360° (all the way round the compass)
> - add to and subtract from 180°

To draw bearings accurately, you must use a ruler and an angle measurer or protractor (although you can use a rough diagram first to help you, like the one below).

Use three digits to measure bearings and measure them clockwise from the North.

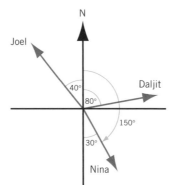

Daljit is walking on a bearing of 080°

Nina is walking on a bearing of 150° (= 180° – 30°)

Joel is walking on a bearing of 320° (= 360° – 40°)

Pythagoras' theorem

In a right-angled triangle, the square of the hypotenuse is equal to squares of the other two sides added together:

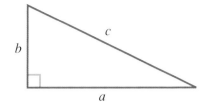

$$c^2 = a^2 + b^2$$

To find a missing side of a right-angled triangle:

Square the two known sides	>	Add to find hypotenuse **or** Subtract to find one of the smaller sides	>	Square root

Trigonometry ratios

Trigonometry is used to calculate the sides and angles in right-angled triangles.

The side opposite the right angle is the hypotenuse (h). It is the longest side.

The side opposite the marked angle (x) is called the opposite (o).

The other side is the adjacent (a).

Remember SOH CAH TOA, to help you decide which formulae to use in trigonometry.

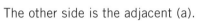

SOH   CAH   TOA

$$\sin x^\circ = \frac{\text{opposite}}{\text{hypotenuse}} \qquad \cos x^\circ = \frac{\text{adjacent}}{\text{hypotenuse}} \qquad \tan x^\circ = \frac{\text{opposite}}{\text{adjacent}}$$

When you need to find one of the sides of a right-angled triangle, use SOC CAH TOA, to get the answer:	opposite = $\sin x$ × hypotenuse adjacent = $\cos x$ × hypotenuse opposite = $\tan x$ × adjacent

EXAMPLE   Find side b.

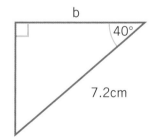

SOLUTION   the adjacent side is b

      7.2cm is the hypotenuse

      Tick off the sides you are concerned with in **SOH CAH TOA**.

      So you will use cos: $\dfrac{\text{adjacent}}{\text{hypotenuse}} = \cos x^\circ$

      adjacent = $\cos x^\circ$ × hypotenuse

      b = $\cos 40^\circ$ × 7.2 = 5.5 cm

GURU TIP

To remember SOH CAH TOA, you could use a mnemonic:

The Old Arab
Sat On His
Camel And Hiccupped
or
Silly Old Harry
Caught A Herring
Trawling Off
Afghanistan
or
Some Old Hags
Can't Always Hide
Their Old Age

GURU TIP

Don't forget to:

* 'square root' to find the solution

* 'add the squares' when finding the smaller sides

* only apply Pythagoras to a right angle triangle.

Algebra

The letters in any algebraic expression are called **variables** and represent numbers. The purpose of using letters is that the numerical value doesn't need to be fixed.

Here are some definitions you should know:

$5y = 20$ is an **equation**	**simplify** = work out like terms
$5t + 3z$ is an **expression**	**expand** = multiply out the brackets
$2x < 10$ is an **inequality**	**factorise** = put in the brackets
	solve an equation = find the value for the letter

EXAMPLE   Given $a = 4$ and $b = 6$ Find $3a + b^2$

SOLUTION   This can be solved by **substitution**. That is the process of replacing the letters by the numerical values you have been given.

$$3a + b^2 = (3 \times 4) + 6^2 = 12 + 36 = 48$$

Terms

- An algebraic expression consisting of only one term is called **monomial**, e.g. $5y$.
- An algebraic expression consisting of two terms is called **binomial**, e.g. $3a + x$.
- A **polynomial** is an algebraic expression consisting of a number of terms, e.g. $y^2 - 4x + 3y + 2$.

Factorisation

To factorise an algebraic expression containing two or more terms, look for the common factors in the expression and then give the original expression in terms of the common factor and a bracket (or two).

EXAMPLE   Factorise $36x + 42y - 24z$

SOLUTION   6 is common to all parts of this expression, so it can be rewritten as:

$$6(6x + 7y - 4z)$$

Algebra often involves brackets and you must be able to remove them too.

EXAMPLE   Simplify $4(2xy + z) - 3(xy - 2z)$

SOLUTION $8xy + 4z - 3xy + 6z = 5xy + 10z$

Simple rules for solving equations

- Always handle both sides of the equation in the same way:
  $x + 6 = 11$ $\Rightarrow$ $x = 11 - 6$ (subtract 6 from both sides) $\Rightarrow$ $x = 5$
- If there are any brackets, multiply them out before you start.
- Remove any fractions by multiplying all terms by the same value:
  $\frac{3x}{4} = 2$ $\Rightarrow$ $3x = 8$ (multiply by 4) $\Rightarrow$ $x = \frac{8}{3}$ $\Rightarrow$ $x = 2\frac{2}{3}$
- Collect all the 'letter' terms on the same side of the equals sign.
  $8y - 3 = 3y + 1$ $\Rightarrow$ $8y - 3y = 1 + 3$ $\Rightarrow$ $5y = 4$ $\Rightarrow$ $y = \frac{4}{5}$

EXAMPLE   Solve $3x - 2 = 2x + 4$

SOLUTION   Move -2 to the right side of the equation, by adding 2 to both sides:

GURU TIP
If you have difficulty, don't panic. Read the question again to check that you are using the correct information. Look for an error in your work. If you can't find one, leave the question and come back to it. Or, if you have time, start again. Don't cross out any of your previous working. You won't lose marks by leaving incorrect working and replacing it with correct working.

GURU TIP
When removing brackets, if the sign before the bracket is positive, the + and − signs inside the bracket stay the same. If the sign before the bracket is negative, the + and − signs inside the bracket change to − and + respectively.

$$3x = 2x + 4 + 2 \quad \Rightarrow \quad 3x = 2x + 6$$

Now move $2x$ to the left side of the equation (by subtracting $2x$ from both sides): $\quad 3x - 2x = 6 \quad \Rightarrow \quad x = 6$

Check the solution by substituting it back in:

$$3x - 2 = 2x + 4 \quad \Rightarrow \quad 3(6) - 2 = 2(6) + 4 \quad \Rightarrow \quad 18 - 2 = 12 + 4 \quad \Rightarrow \quad 16 = 16 \checkmark$$

Simultaneous equations

Look at the equation $x + 3y = 7$. It is called a linear equation in x and y. On its own like this, we can't do much to find out the value of x and y. But if we have a second similar equation, we can work out the value of x and y to satisfy the two equations worked together (simultaneously).

EXAMPLE Solve: $\quad x + y = 2$ (i) $\quad 2x + y = 3$ (ii)

SOLUTION by **elimination**

Deal with it term by term. Subtract (i) from (ii).

First the x terms and y terms and then the numbers

$$(2x - x) + (y - y) = 3 - 2$$

So the solution is $x = 1$

Substitute the value of x into either of the original equations to find the value of y:

$$x + y = 2 \quad \Rightarrow \quad 1 + y = 2 \quad \Rightarrow \quad y = 2 - 1 \quad \Rightarrow \quad y = 1$$

So the solution is $x = 1$, $y = 1$

You can also solve it by **substitution**. In this case you rewrite equation (i) to make one of the variables (x or y) the subject:

$$x + y = 2 \quad \Rightarrow \quad y = 2 - x$$

Now substitute the rearranged equation (i) into equation (ii):

$$2x + y = 3 \quad \Rightarrow \quad 2x + (2 - x) = 3 \quad \Rightarrow \quad 2x + 2 - x = 3 \quad \Rightarrow \quad x + 2 = 3$$

This gives $x = 3 - 2$, so $x = 1$

Substitute the value of x into either of the original equations to find the value of y:

$$x + y = 2 \quad \Rightarrow \quad 1 + y = 2 \quad \Rightarrow \quad y = 2 - 1 \quad \Rightarrow \quad y = 1$$

So the solution is $x = 1$, $y = 1$

Rearranging formulae

The subject of a formula is the letter that usually appears on the left-hand side of the equals sign, by itself. If you have to rearrange the formula to get another subject, you must 'undo' all the operations on the new subject. It is often useful to use a simple flow chart for this.

EXAMPLE Make u the subject of this formula: $\quad v^2 = u^2 + 2as$

SOLUTION

| u | → | squared | → | add $2as$ | → | v^2 |

| v^2 | → | subtract $2as$ | → | square rooted | → | u |

Therefore the new formula is $u = \sqrt{v^2 - 2as}$

Simultaneous equations can also be solved graphically. Lines are drawn to represent each equation, the point at which the lines cross is the solution.

GURU TIP
Always check your answers by substituting the numbers into one of the equations.

GURU TIP
If you substitute values into the original equation to find the value of the subject, then the values must work for the rearranged formula. However, avoid 0, 1 and 2 as these numbers have special properties. For this example:

$u = 8$ $a = 3$ $s = 6$ gives $v = 10$

$$8 = \sqrt{10^2 - 2 \times 3 \times 6}$$

Statistics

The maths skills covered by statistics are widely used in everyday life. The ability to understand how a variety of statistical values are found and their use when comparing two or more sets of data is very important.

Sampling methods

In statistics you study data obtained from observation, experiments, questionnaires or interviews.

When data is collected, it is rare for the whole population to be taken into account. To find out about the whole population, for example in the 10-year nationwide census, is expensive and time consuming. So, instead we take a sample of the population and gather the data from that. In order to draw conclusions about the whole population from the sample data, you must choose the sample very carefully.

This is called a 'random sample', meaning that every member of the population has an equal chance of being selected in the sample.

With a **simple random sample,** every element of the population to be sampled has an equally likely chance of being picked. Often, each element is assigned a number and the numbers are chosen at random.

With a **stratified random sample,** each sub-group of a population is represented in the correct proportion in a sample. Opinion pollsters, such as Gallup and Mori, claim to use this method.

EXAMPLE   A sample of 100 people is to be taken from a population for a survey. How many people should be questioned from each village?

	Population
Village A	425
Village B	575
Village C	250
Village D	350

$\frac{425}{1600}$ is the fraction of the population from Village A

SOLUTION   The total population = 425 + 575 + 250 + 350 = 1600

Sample from Village A = $\frac{425}{1600} \times 100 = 26.56$ so round up to 27 people

Sample from Village B = $\frac{575}{1600} \times 100 = 35.9$ so round up to 36 people

(For more on rounding up and down, see page 37.)

Questionnaires

Most surveys for car-makers, supermarkets and so on, use questionnaires. Questionnaires should ensure that people are honest. The questions must be unbiased, easy to analyse and simple to understand. They should not be vague or leading.

Questionnaires should have an introduction so that the subject knows the purpose of the questions.

GURU TIP
In a sample the following things are important:

- **size** – is it large enough?
- **representative** – does it represent all points of view?
- **random** – do all subjects have an equal chance of being chosen?

GURU TIP
There is a good way to memorise what is important in a survey:

It should not be **a**mbiguous or **l**eading. It should **i**nclude all responses possible. It should not be **b**iased.

If you don't remember this, you won't have an alibi!

Mean, median and mode

The average is the central value of the data collected. The three types of averages most commonly used are the **mean**, **median** and **mode**.

	How calculated	Advantages	Disadvantages
Mean	Sum of all the data divided by the number of items of data.	Most commonly used measure of 'average'. Used in more complex statistical measures.	Very high/low items of data distort the mean value.
Median	Data is ordered from the smallest to the largest. The median is the item of data in the middle.	Easy to calculate and may give a physical example of the 'average' item of data.	Data must be numerical.
Mode	The item which occurs most often in a set of data.	Easy to find. Can be found for data that is not numerical. Very useful in manufacturing/retail.	Certain sets of data may not give a modal value. Some will give two or more modes. Not used widely.

There are more sophisticated statistical measures of spread.
See page 47 for information on cumulative frequency curves and the interquartile range.

Maths

Spread or range

> **Spread or range = largest value – smallest value**

The spread of a set of data is a basic indication of how uniform the items of data are. If a group of people were asked their age, a small range would be expected if the survey was carried out in a junior school playground, whereas a larger range would be expected if the survey took place in a shopping centre on a Saturday afternoon.

Together with either the mean, median or mode, the spread of a set of data can be used to make predictions or decisions based on statistical data.

KEY SKILLS N3.1

EXAMPLE A fourth member of a school swimming team is needed for the relay. Ben and Sean are available. It is estimated that, to win the race, the fourth member of the team needs to record a time of 55 seconds. Data shows the following:

Ben	Mean time = 57 seconds	Range = 4 seconds
Sean	Mean time = 58 seconds	Range = 10 seconds

Who would you choose?

SOLUTION Ben has the best mean time, but a smaller range indicates that his times will probably be 57 sec +/– 2 sec, so, at best, 55 sec and at worst 59 sec.

Sean's results show a slower mean, but his range suggests he is probably capable of times 58 sec +/– 5 sec, that is between 53 sec and 63 sec.

Ben could achieve 55 sec with one of his best performances, Sean could easily achieve 55 seconds but is equally likely to record a much slower time than Ben.

KEY SKILLS
To obtain Key Skill N3.1, perform two surveys. One on your class mates and one on shoppers or friends. By asking the same questions, you can compare the data, using different averages.

GURU TIP
You can draw conclusions from your work, but you need to make sure you can justify them with evidence. So your answer could be Ben, or Sean, but you would need to justify your choice with reference to the data.

Functions and graphs

GURU TIP
Remember that all the angles in a cricle give a total of 360° and all the percentages of a group total 100%.

KEY SKILLS
Once you have collected your data, use a computer to produce useful graphs for a presentation that compares your results.

KEY SKILLS
IT3

The data you record can be **discrete** or **continuous**. Discrete data can take only certain values, such as the number of children in a class. Continuous data comes from measuring and can take any value and range, such as the time taken to drink a milkshake.

Once the data has been collected, the next stage is to classify and tabulate it. For example, in the workplace many employees spend time recording data in order to analyse it for their future work. Manual and computerised record-keeping will also help with your planning and projects.

Pie charts show information in the form of a circle.

This pie chart shows methods of transport to work (40 people surveyed).

360° or 100% represents the whole sample, in other words 40 people are represented by 360°.

So 1 person = $\frac{360°}{40}$ = 9°

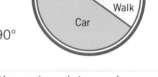

EXAMPLE   How many people travel to work by bus?

SOLUTION   The section representing travel by bus is 90°

90° ÷ 9° = 10 people

A **line graph** is a way of showing information so that the main points can be seen easily and the patterns are clear.

EXAMPLE   In a talent competition the judges award the contestants marks out of 5. Show this information in graphical form.

```
1 3 2 3 4 2
1 3 0 5 3 0
1 4 0 4 4 3
3 4 3 1 3 4
3 1 2 1 3 4
0 4 3 2 5 3
```

Mark	Tally	Frequency
0	IIII	4
1	HHT I	6
2	IIII	4
3	HHT HHT II	12
4	HHT III	8
5	II	2

SOLUTION   You can use a line graph to show this data, as there is no range of values in each case, just a specific number of marks.

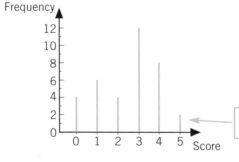

The length of each line represents how often the corresponding mark occurs.

The mark of 5 occurs twice.

A **bar chart** is another way to illustrate data. The height of each bar shows the frequency. Like line graphs, bar charts are used to show discrete data.

There should be gaps between the bars.

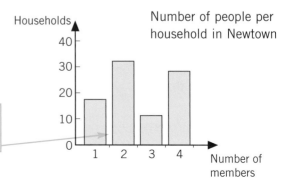

Number of people per household in Newtown

A **histogram** is used to illustrate data with continuous value, i.e. with values that change all the time, for example the height of a plant. The data is grouped into class intervals. There are no gaps between the groups.

EXAMPLE   The weekly salaries of 40 employees are shown in the table on the right.

SOLUTION   These data can be shown in a histogram with the height of the rectangles showing each class interval.

Wages	Number of employees
£200–209	5
£210–219	6
£220–229	10
£230–239	15
£240–249	4

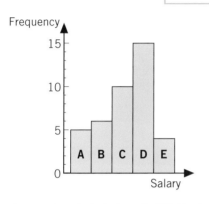

the height of A is 5 units

the height of B is 6 units

the height of C is 10 units

the height of D is 15 units

the height of E is 4 units

GURU TIP
In histograms, if the bars are of different widths, the area of the bar (not the height) represents the frequency.

Maths

Frequency polygons are drawn by joining the mid-points of the top of each rectangle in a histogram. Here is the same histogram, redrawn as a frequency polygon.

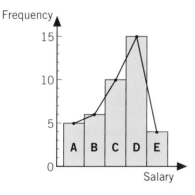

Frequency polygons give the general shape of a distribution.

Frequency polygons are often used to compare two or more sets of information about similar data.

Look at this example which shows age distribution in two villages.

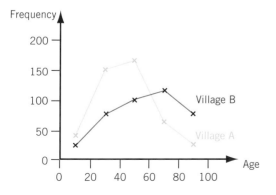

From the frequency polygon, you can see that the proportion of people under 50 is larger in Village A.

Functions and graphs continued

GURU TIP

- Make the title of charts and graphs clear – what is the data about, where is it from and when was it collected?

- Any columns and rows should be labelled.

- Give the degree of accuracy of any approximate data.

Sometimes you might be interested in finding out if there is a relationship (correlation) between two sets of data, for example do tall parents have tall children, and if you spend longer revising will you get a higher mark in the exam?

Scatter diagrams look for a correlation between two sets of data. One set of data is plotted on the horizontal axis and the other is plotted on the vertical axis.

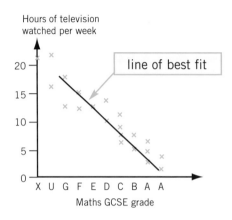

Here, the line of best fit has been drawn 'by eye'. It connects as many of the plotted points as possible. The line has a negative gradient. So you say there is a negative correlation. So the hours of TV watched per week does not increase the maths GCSE grade.

Making the correlation

- Points that are close to the line have a strong correlation.

- Points that are further away from the line have a weak correlation.

- Positive correlation slopes upwards.

- Negative correlation slopes downwards.

Look at these scatter diagrams.

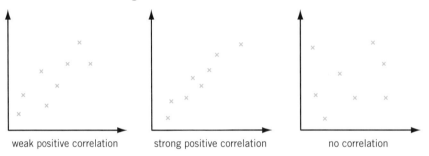

Conversion graphs illustrate the link between two sets of data. They can be linked by an algebraic formula. Conversion graphs do not have to go through the origin, although they often do. They can be straight lines or curves.

A straight line with a positive gradient shows that one set of data is proportional to the other set of data.

> $y = mx + c$ is the equation of a straight line
>
> m is the **gradient** and c is the **interception** on the vertical axis

This example shows the exchange rate for the Mexican Peso. Therefore:

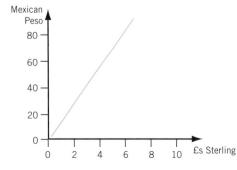

Mexican Peso = 13.2 × Pounds Sterling + 0

(correct exchange rate on 21 January 2001)

Cumulative frequency curves help with calculations of the distribution.

It is easy to find the median from the halfway point and other points can also be located on the curve.

The cumulative frequency axis can be divided into 100 parts or percentiles.

The upper quartile is at the 75% point – that is the 75th percentile.
The lower range is at the 25% point – that is the 25th percentile.

Percentiles are ways of locating particular positions on a curve.

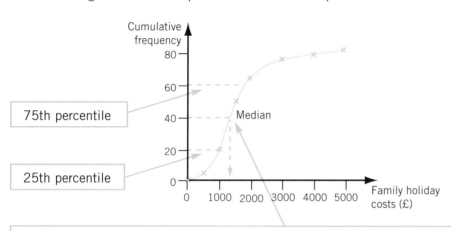

Median = half of frequency

To find the median (average) value use the curve (sometimes called an 'ogive'). Find the number which divides the distribution into 2 equal parts with equal frequencies. Here a frequency of 40 gives a median value which can be read off as £1,375.

The intermediate range or the **interquartile range** is an important measure of spread as it shows how widely the data is spread.
The range is found by reading off the 75th and 25th percentiles.

interquartile range = 75th percentile – 25th percentile

EXAMPLE   Find the interquartile range of the cumulative frequency curve above.

SOLUTION   The 75th percentile is 1,875

The 25th percentile is 1,000

So the range is 1,875 – 1000 = 875

GURU TIP
Always study any graph or chart carefully before you answer a question about it.

- Look at the axes – what do they represent, are the scales clear, what is the scale on each axis?

- Do the scales start at zero? If not, the chart may be misleading, indicating a large increase or decrease in a quantity when only a small change actually occurs.

Maths

Probability

Probability is a way of using maths to estimate the chance that an event will happen. In a raffle, you buy a ticket in the hope that you will win. If you buy 2 of 100 tickets, you will have a 2 in 100 chance of winning. If you do not buy a ticket at all, your chance of winning will be 0 in 100, or impossible. If you buy all the tickets, it will be 100 in 100, or a certainty.

GURU WEBSITE
Visit the AS Guru™ website at www.bbc.co.uk/asguru for more on probability.

What are probabilities used for?	
Conducting a survey or experiment	You suspect that a coin is biased, it seems to land on heads more than tails. A simple experiment would find the probability of landing on heads.
Looking at data	Used by weather forecasters and insurance companies. Data shows that you are more likely to have your car broken into in towns and cities, thus insurance premiums are higher for those drivers who live in a town or city.
Subjective estimate	This is used when the event is not repeatable. To work out the probability of a horse winning the Derby (only 2-year-old horses can enter this race) would require looking at previous races the horse has entered, but conditions on the day and the form of other horses will play a factor in the outcome.

Most of the questions on probability you will encounter in the exam will involve games of chance, for example throwing a dice, cutting a normal pack of cards or tossing a coin.

$$\text{Probability an event happens} = \frac{\text{number of successful ways the event can happen}}{\text{number of outcomes possible}}$$

For example, the probability a red King will be cut from a pack of cards $= \dfrac{2}{52}$

In maths, probabilities are given as fractions. Sometimes they can be given as decimals or percentages.

If all the outcomes of a particular event are known, their probabilities will add up to 1. So the probability of something happening is the same as 1 minus the probability that it will not happen.

GURU TIP
Probabilities should never be given as odds, such as 3 in 5; this is a common error and will lose marks in an examination.

> P (event happens) = 1 – P (all the ways that it will not happen)

EXAMPLE The probability that a certain football team will win the next match it plays is 0.56, the probability of a draw is 0.38. What is the probability it will lose?

SOLUTION Probability the team will lose = 1 – 0.56 – 0.38 = 0.06

Using probabilities, you can estimate the number of times an event will happen if you know the total number of times the experiment will take place.

> Expected number of successes = probability of success × number of trials

EXAMPLE The probability of being left handed is $\frac{1}{7}$.

In an exam room with 150 candidates how many left-handed students would you expect?

SOLUTION Expected number of left-handed candidates = $\frac{1}{7}$ × 150 = 21

If you want to find the probability of drawing a red card or the King of clubs from a pack of cards, you can use a Venn diagram.

The sample space (that is the full set of all possible events) consists of 52 events. There are 52 cards in the pack.

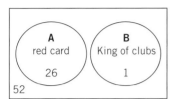

A There are 26 red cards in the pack = $\frac{26}{52}$

B There is 1 King of clubs in the pack = $\frac{1}{52}$

A and B are **mutually exclusive**. Mutually exclusive events cannot occur at the same time. You cannot pick a red card at the same time as picking the King of Clubs, because the King of clubs is a black card.

You can work it out as: $\boxed{\text{P(A or B) = P(A) + P(B)}}$

So the probability (of a red card or King of clubs) = $\frac{26}{52} + \frac{1}{52} = \frac{27}{52}$

When are events not mutually exclusive?

Look at this Venn diagram. It is to work out the probability of drawing a Queen or a Heart from a pack of 52 cards.

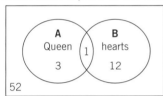

There are 13 hearts in the pack (set B) and 4 Queens (set B). The Queen of hearts is contained in both sets, the sets intersect.

Probability of hearts P(B) = $\frac{13}{52} = \frac{1}{4}$ Probability of Queen P(A) = $\frac{4}{12} = \frac{1}{3}$

Probability of Queen or heart = P(A or B) = $\frac{12 + 1 + 3}{52} = \frac{16}{52} = \frac{4}{13}$

Conditional probability
What if you are asked the probability of drawing a red card if it is known that an Ace is drawn? This reduces the sample space as there are only 4 Aces in a pack. The chances of the Ace selected being a red card is $\frac{2}{4} = \frac{1}{2}$

Independent events
Two events are independent if they do not affect the outcome of each other. They are usually two separate events, for example selecting a red card from a pack of cards (A) and tossing a coin and getting a head (B).

When these two events (A and B) are independent, the probability of both A and B happening is: $\boxed{\text{P(A and B) = P(A) × P(B)}}$

EXAMPLE   What is the probability of selecting a red card from a pack of cards and tossing a coin and getting a head?

SOLUTION   Red card = $\frac{26}{52}$ Coin on heads = $\frac{1}{2}$

= $\frac{26}{52} \times \frac{1}{2} = \frac{26}{104} = \frac{1}{4}$

When you multiply two fractions that are smaller than 1, the result is smaller than the two original fractions. In terms of probability, this is consistent: the probability that two events will happen must be smaller than the probability that either one of them will happen.

Maths

This is known as the multiplication law of probability.

Algorithms and networks

Algorithms were first discussed by the Arab mathematician Al-Khwarizmi. Many believe that 'algorithm' was named after a King or Prince who decreed that calculations must be carried out according to the laws he set out. Now the word is used for a specific routine for solving a particular problem, for example you will have learnt algorithms for doing addition or long division or for finding the square root.

One of the new areas of mathematics to emerge over recent decades is called Decision Mathematics, in which you use mathematical skills to provide information. This can be used to decide how you are going to run a project, where to invest money to make a company more efficient, or even where the best position for a fire station would be. These questions require advanced skills in Decision Mathematics. Here, you are just going to look at some of the basic principles.

Algorithms

These are systematic processes which, when repeated a number of times, will produce the answer to a given problem. They can be given in words or in the form of a flowchart.

EXAMPLE The ISBN (International Standard Book Number) is used to classify every book published. There are ten digits in the ISBN. The first 9 are used to reference the book and the last digit is a check digit. Find the check digit for the BBC publication GCSE Bitesize Revision Maths if the 9 figure reference number is: ISBN 0 563 46119 ....

SOLUTION
- First multiply the first digit by 1, the second by 2, the third by 3 ... and so on until you multiply the ninth digit by 9.

- Add together all the results of these calculations.

- Divide the sum by 11 and record the remainder. If the remainder is 0 to 9 then this is the check digit, if the remainder is 10 the check digit is X. So the check digit in this question is 5:

ISBN 0 563 46119 5

First fit algorithm

Imagine you have a set of bins in which you can pack boxes. The boxes are the same width and length as the bins, only the heights differ. This algorithm deals with how to fit as many boxes as possible into the bins in a systematic way.

> **Algorithm**
> Take the boxes in the order listed, place the next box to be packed in the first bin with space that the box will fit into. This algorithm can be refined by putting the boxes into order of size, starting with the tallest.

GURU TIP
If there is a question on algorithms, the examiner is looking for your ability to follow instructions carefully and work through problems in a logical manner.

The algorithm can be used in a variety of situations, for example loading vehicles onto a ferry or deciding how many planks of wood are required for a job that needs a number of different sized pieces.

EXAMPLE How many 3-hour tapes will be needed to video programmes of the following lengths?

2.5 hours	1 hour	30 minutes	45 minutes
1.5 hours	30 minutes	2 hours	1.5 hours
45 minutes	2 hours	50 minutes	40 minutes

SOLUTION Label the programmes:

A: 2.5 hours	B: 1 hour	C: 30 minutes	D: 45 minutes
E: 1.5 hours	F: 30 minutes	G: 2 hours	H: 1.5 hours
I: 45 minutes	J: 2 hours	K: 50 minutes	L: 40 minutes

Tape 1	A, C	Programme A goes on the first tape, B will not fit on this tape and so needs to go on tape 2.
Tape 2	B, D, F, I	Programme C fits in the remaining space on Tape 1.
Tape 3	E, H	Continue to decide if there is sufficient space on each tape in order for each programme.
Tape 4	G, K	
Tape 5	H, L	
Tape 6	J	

If the programmes had been put in order, longest to shortest first, A, G, J, E, H, B, K, D, I, L, C, F, one tape fewer would have been needed.

Networks

Networks use diagrams linking points (called nodes) with lines (called arcs) to give a simple picture to represent a more complicated system.

EXAMPLE This network represents the distances between certain towns.

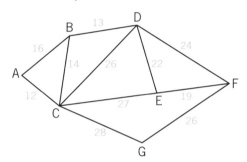

A cable television company wants to connect all the towns using the minimum amount of cable. What is the optimum solution for this?

GURU TIP
Think of familiar networks:
- the London Underground map
- chemical structure diagrams
- electrical circuit diagrams.

SOLUTION

Algorithm

Step 1 List all edges in order of length.

Step 2 Select the shortest edge in the network.

Step 3 From the edges not already used, select the shortest that does not connect two towns already connected.

Step 4 Repeat step 3 until all towns are connected.

Arcs in order: AC = 12 1st connector = AC

BD = 13 2nd connector = BD

BC = 14 3rd connector = BC

AB = 16 4th connector = EF (not AB since A is already connected to B via C)

EF = 19

DE = 22 5th connector = DE

DF = 24 6th connector = GF (DF is connected via E)

CD = 26 (CD is connected via B)

GF = 26

CE = 27

CG = 28

Minimum amount of cable = 12 + 13 + 14 + 19 + 22 + 26 = 106

You can use network diagrams to solve many practical questions.

- How do you get from one point to another in the shortest time or distance?

- Which route should a gritter take to cover every road in a town as quickly as possible?

Practice questions

1 In a pie chart representing the total annual costs of BATS plc, the angle representing advertising is 130°. If the total cost for everything except advertising is £3 600 000, what is the cost of advertising to the nearest £1000?

2 The probability that it will be wet today is 0.7. If it is dry today, the probability that it will be wet tomorrow is 0.4. What is the probability that it will be dry today and tomorrow?

3 The following vehicles are waiting to board the Windermere ferry. The list includes the length of each vehicle. Read along the rows.

Van 3 m	Coach 12 m	Car 3 m	Car 3 m
Truck 8 m	Lorry 12 m	Car 4 m	Coach 10 m
Car 3 m	Van 4 m	Car 3 m	Car 3 m

How many vehicles can the ferry load if it has three lanes each 20 m long?

If the vehicles are ordered in size, largest first (in the same way that large cross-channel ferries operate) could any more vehicles be loaded?

4 A TV costs £345 after a reduction of 20%. What was its original cost?

5 Work out the difference between one ton and one tonne.
   1 tonne = 1000kg   1 ton = 2240lb   1lb = 454g

6 A boat sails 80km due south and 100km due east. On what bearing must the boat sail to return to its starting point and how far will it need to sail in this direction?

7 A local newspaper wanted to estimate the number of people who bought its paper in a certain town. It telephoned 50 people in the town and asked 'Have you read the Standard in the last month?' Thirteen people said 'Yes', so the newspaper claimed that 26% of the population bought the paper. Give three criticisms of this method of estimation.

8 The sum of the first n integers is given by the formula:

   $s^n = 2 \div n(1 + n)$

   Use the formula to find the sum of the first 50 integers.

   Then find the value of 20 + 21 + 22 + 23 +. . .+ 49 + 50

9 The following network represents the distances between seven towns. Find the shortest distance to travel from Town A to Town G.

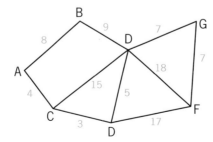

Science and Technology

In this section you will learn about:

☞ how scientists think and work

☞ examples of major scientific advances

☞ some of the major scientific issues facing the world today

☞ how science and technology can benefit and harm society.

If you're studying AS General Studies you'll need to know a little science. We live in a modern, technological society where scientists can perform what would have been called miracles in the Middle Ages. You'll already know plenty of science from GCSE. You might also be studying one or more sciences at AS level, but you'll be affected by science and technology in your everyday life:

- when you use a computer to send emails or surf the web
- when you turn on the TV to watch the latest soap or drama
- if you take antibiotics to cure an infection
- when you turn on a light
- when you read a newspaper or watch the news.

It doesn't matter if you weren't inspired by GCSE science or had problems getting your head around moles or balancing equations. This isn't the focus of AS General Studies. The issues discussed in this section are some that you will need to face in the future, so it's wise to get informed about them now. If you're a scientist then that's a bonus and you can use your detailed knowledge, but if you're not scientifically minded then it's not a problem – this is about people and issues.

The key to being successful in this area of AS General Studies is similar to the rest of the course. You need to develop your own points of view about genetically engineered food, nuclear power and environmental issues, for example. Your arguments should show that you are aware and can take account of other people's views. A balanced answer, demonstrating an understanding of a range of opinions will gain more marks than just writing about your own ideas. If you can back up answers with specific examples then that's even better and will impress examiners.

Science and technology is continually changing and you need to take account of this. Many new ideas came to light while this book was being written and scientific issues are bound to have developed further. As you read this section:

- make sure you understand both sides of the argument
- think about how the issues affect your life and what you think about them
- research issues that you're interested in or not sure about
- keep an eye on the news and read quality papers or popular science magazines to keep up to date with new advances.

What is science?

At the most basic level, science is the knowledge gained and the methods used to for acquiring further knowledge. This depends on observation, experimentation, and the use of specific theories to explain natural phenomena.

Scientists try to understand how natural phenomena work and put forward a suggested explanation, based on their experiments. However, this means that all scientific knowledge is theoretically able to be proved wrong. If it can't be proved wrong then it's not science – which is why scientists can't answer questions, such as 'Is there a God?' Science can help reach philosophical conclusions on supernatural issues, but can't actually test them.

How do scientists work?

There are two basic ways in which scientists can work, although only one of these is generally accepted as 'scientific method':

- using **induction** to build scientific knowledge
- **creative insight**.

Induction is a form of argument based on direct observation. From observation, scientists can generalise about natural phenomena. Galileo's observations about the Solar System led him to test and validate the hypothesis put forward by the Polish astronomer, Copernicus, that the Earth orbits the Sun. He rejected the arguments put forward by Aristotle that the Earth was at the centre of the universe.

Creative insight is the jump to a conclusion without the direct observation. It is the sudden realisation of a scientific theory that could then be tested by using inductive methods. Copernicus' original work was more creative. He made measurements but couldn't check his theory that the Sun was the centre of the Solar System.

Creative insight can lead to sudden advances in scientific knowledge. Induction is generally a slower process, due to the direct observation and testing required. It usually requires a series of smaller steps to reach the same end result. Although both methods may be used by scientists, modern scientific method is based on induction, rather than creative insight.

Scientific method depends on a series of steps, such as observation, forming a hypothesis, analysis, validation and conclusion.

Observation
Start by observing a phenomenon and looking for patterns. For example, the cars on the high street drive on the left-hand side of the road.

Hypothesis
Based on the observations, form a hypothesis – a blanket statement on the universal behaviour of the phenomenon: all cars drive on the left-hand side of the road.

Analysis
Through observation and analysis, identify and clearly state a problem to be solved or question to be answered. In this case, the analysis could take place at 1000 random locations and investigate which side of the road people drive on. Repeat this many times to prevent any strange occurrences distorting the results.

Validation
Test the statistics to see if the results are reliable and if they support the hypothesis.

Conclusion
Accept or reject the hypothesis on the basis of the outcome of the experiments.

GURU TIP
Galileo Galilee was born in Pisa, Italy, on 4 May 1564. He was a famous physicist, writer and astronomer and designed the light telescope.

GURU WEBSITE
Test your science and technology general knowledge. Visit the General Studies section of the AS Guru™ website at www.bbc.co.uk/asguru and take the scientific discovery test. The Guru will collect your scores throughout the course, so you can track your progress.

Testing theories

Once a hypothesis is accepted or rejected it must be repeatable – others must also be able to test it. Only if it can be tested can a theory be accepted as steadfast scientific knowledge.

Once a hypothesis has been accepted, it can be challenged through the same process. Scientists use analysis and observation to question the hypothesis (based upon observations which would seem not to fit) and to propose alternative hypotheses that are then able to be validated through more testing. In this way, scientific knowledge and understanding can be moved on and scientific advances can be made.

Importantly, underlying all science is the principle that scientific conclusions are tentative, not the final word. Any conclusion, which we now hold to be true, may later be proved incorrect by testing against the world around us. If a theory is never proved wrong then we assume that it is a fact. Although it's hard to imagine future scientists proving that oxygen is bad for human beings or that gravity doesn't keep our feet on the ground, it is possible. It's easier to imagine that rather more tentative scientific beliefs could be challenged.

GURU TV
Professor Joseph Rotblat won the Nobel Peace Prize in 1996. Listen to what he's got to say about the moral and ethical implications of scientific research.

Current use of the scientific method

Sudden Infant Death Syndrome (SIDS) is the most common cause of infant deaths in developed countries. Over the years there have been many suggested causes of SIDS:

- fungus on a baby's mattress
- carbon dioxide building up around the baby's face, affecting the breathing
- parents who smoke
- lying babies on their stomach.

A recent study suggests that babies who die from this syndrome could be infected with a common bacterium, called *Helicobacter pylori*. It has been suggested that *Helicobacter* might lead to the production of ammonia in a baby's lungs.

In a study of 32 babies who died of SIDS, doctors in Manchester have found that almost 90% were infected with the bacterium. To the non-scientist this may sound like a pretty convincing result. However, although the study is statistically significant, the number of cases studied is quite small. The researchers say more work is needed to confirm their results.

This is an example of scientific development in action.

Jenner

Edward Jenner is credited with the invention of the modern vaccination theory. He is famous for developing a vaccine for smallpox – a deadly and potentially disfiguring disease. Jenner noticed that dairy farmers, milk maids and others who worked with cows were particularly prone to contracting cowpox, but they never suffered from smallpox. Jenner believed that by contracting and recovering from cowpox, these people had developed a protection against smallpox. In 1796, he inoculated a young boy with cowpox cells. The patient recovered from the non-fatal infection and was then injected with smallpox but failed to contract the disease. On one hand, Jenner's hypothesis – that cowpox provided protection against infection from smallpox – was proved correct through testing. On the other hand, however, his work was not proven, in the sense that he didn't actually see the antibodies formed as protection against the cowpox and how these fought the smallpox infection.

Jenner's work involved inductive thought. This is a good example of someone who followed scientific methodology and formed the basis of our current thoughts on inoculation.

Science and technology

Evolutionary theories

GURU TIP

The Big Bang theory is a scientific theory to explain the origin of the universe. The Big Bang is thought to have created the universe, 10–20 billion years ago from a cosmic explosion.

In your GCSE science lessons you probably learnt about **evolution** – the idea that life evolved and adapted over millions of years, and will continue developing.

In General Studies you will need a basic understanding of evolution and the evidence used to back up this important scientific idea. You can also use evolution as an example of how scientists develop their theories and ideas.

In many ways, all science is underpinned by the theory of evolution:

- the rock cycle assumes that rocks were created over millions of years and continue to be destroyed and created in the same way
- different parts of plants have evolved to do a particular job. Sunken cacti **stomata** have developed to prevent water loss by evaporation
- the Big Bang theory suggests that life evolved from basic building blocks.

As well as scientific ideas, you also need to know about influential scientists. Check out the profile of Charles Darwin on page 59 and use the Internet and reference books to find out similar information on people who have had a big impact on the scientific world (see page 59 for some ideas on who to research).

Evolution in action

GURU TIP

The ideas behind evolution are often linked to other scientific theories, such as the Big Bang theory. However, they are separate – you don't have to believe in the Big Bang theory to believe in evolution. Check out the section on **creationism** on page 58 for more information on this.

The ideas on which Darwin's ideas were based, developed over a long period of time. They have not stood still either, continuing to evolve as scientists push forward their understanding. Below, is a brief outline of some key evolutionary ideas that helped give rise to Darwin's theory of evolution.

Ancient China
Confucius – life originated from a single source, through gradual development.

Greek and Medieval period
Empedocles – action of elemental forces gave rise to life (basis of organic evolution).

Aristotle – proposed continuous development of animals, based on observations.

Age of speculation (1400–1790)
Carl Linnaeus – suggested that species were variants of common groups of animals or plants that had developed.

Age of formulation (1790–1900)
Jean-Baptiste Lamarck believed that the environment caused adaptations in individuals, such as an elephant becoming stronger, and that these adaptations would be passed onto offspring. This helped form a basis for Darwin's theories.

Charles Lyell found fossil evidence to support a progressive history, providing a foundation for Darwin's ideas.

Charles Darwin developed the theory of evolution by **natural selection**.

Alfred Russell Wallace co-operated with Darwin, promoting several similar ideas before the publication of *Origins*. Darwin often gets credit for using Wallace's work.

Gregor Mendel's work on genetics helped develop the laws of inheritance.

Twentieth Century developments
Scientists continue to argue about the mechanics of evolution. In particular, whether it occurs by natural selection or by **random genetic mutation**.

Watson and Crick discovered the physical structure of **DNA**.

Does everyone believe in evolution?

Evolution is only a theory, but one that most scientists agree on. Given that it is generally taken for granted, you might be surprised to discover that:

- until 1968 it was illegal to teach evolution in many US states
- in a recent survey, a third of Americans wanted creationism to be taught as a science in schools, with 16% wanting evolution not to be taught at all
- in 1999, Kansas banned the teaching of evolution, removing all references to both evolution and the Big Bang theory of the origins of the universe from school work.

The Big Bang theory suggests that the universe began to form millions of years ago from hot, dense matter, which has been expanding ever since. It's an example of a complicated scientific paradigm (see below) that scientists have trouble proving. Quite what the universe is expanding into is something that scientists can't answer right now – but they'll let you know if they ever get there!

What is a paradigm?

A **paradigm** is more than a theory. There can be lots of different theories. Paradigms are more central in that they direct the ways in which scientists will try to develop theories. The advantage of this is that everyone has a set of rules they work from that everyone else understands. It's easier to make progress if the same rules are used by everyone.

The concept of a paradigm was developed in the 1960s, by Thomas Kuhn. Kuhn (1922–1996) was an American historian of science who was interested in why scientists think and work in the way they do. He suggested that there was a set of beliefs in a particular area that scientists would agree on, at any one time. These beliefs underpinned scientists' work and provided them with the assumptions they needed to study science. Kuhn used this concept to explain why scientific revolutions come about – periods when the basic beliefs changed rapidly. He called this a paradigm shift, where the existing paradigm is seen to be inadequate and a new one is developed.

At present, evolution is a paradigm that most scientists accept as scientific 'fact'. But this wasn't always the case. Until 1859, the religious paradigm of creationism (explained over the page) was generally accepted as the explanation of the development of the Earth and the species living on it. The evolution paradigm was first proposed, in print, in 1859 by Charles Darwin (see page 59) and was considered a very controversial theory.

What do you think?

Is evolution science fact? Most scientists will tell you it is. It's certainly the dominant paradigm when it comes to looking at how species develop over time. Remember, you need to be able to use evolution as an example of the development of a paradigm, and be able to provide evidence to support it and question it.

GURU TIP
It's worth knowing that scientists have various theories as to how evolution actually works, though all of these agree that evolution does occur. Don't worry, you won't be expected to know the details of these theories – unless you're particularly interested.

Science and technology

Evolution and creation

What is evolution?

In its simplest form, evolution is the changes in the gene pool of a population. It's how plants and animals adapt over a long period of time. In any species there is variation – some giraffes are taller and some are shorter. The taller ones can reach more food than the smaller ones and are therefore better able to survive periods of food shortage. These are the 'best' giraffes – they have an advantage that the shorter giraffes don't. Charles Darwin (see page 59) suggested that these 'better' giraffes were more likely to survive and pass their characteristics on to their offspring. This is known as 'survival of the fittest', or natural selection and explains why giraffes have long necks.

Evidence to support the theory of evolution

- Species have been observed to evolve – for example, peppered moths in Britain have become darker over the last 200 years, as industrial pollution increased, being darker made it easier for the moths to camouflage themselves in a pollution-blackened habitat. In industrial areas, lighter moths were eaten more rapidly, while darker ones survived to breed. This shows the moths adapting to new conditions. In less polluted areas, the reverse is true, and there is a greater concentration of lighter-coloured moths.

- Bacteria are continually mutating into new strains that can resist drugs – the 'superbugs' that are resistant to antibiotics, for example.

- Fossil records suggest that species have evolved slowly over millions of years. Fossils show that small changes have taken place over time, to result in the species seen today. Fossil remains of early humans show similarities to modern people and suggest that there are links between today's humans and those from ancient times.

What is creationism?

Creationism is the belief that the universe was created by a god. This does not have to be at odds with the theories of evolution proposed by Darwin. It is possible to believe that the world was created by a god or gods, who then allowed life to evolve. Fundamental Christian creationists believe that the world is less than 10 000 years old and was literally created in six days. These groups usually take the Bible as direct evidence for this and interpret it exactly as it is written.

Creationists maintain that you don't have to believe in the Big Bang theory to accept evolution. They believe that the universe came into being, but nature was left to take its course – that's evolution. You can argue that the universe developed naturally (in which case what was here beforehand?) or that it was somehow created.

Creationism is still proposed as a major theory by some groups.

Evidence to support creationism

- Fundamental creationists argue that living beings were created in their current form and that no major changes have occurred since the creation.

- They argue that any evidence for evolution has simply been created by the creator in order to test our belief in religion.

- Creationists suggest that scientists cannot prove evolution.

Charles Darwin 12th February 1809 – 19th April 1882

Education:

Shrewsbury School

Edinburgh University – student of medicine

Cambridge University – theology student.

In 1831, Darwin accepted an invitation to take part in a five year scientific voyage to South America on HMS Beagle as an unpaid naturalist.

A lot of Darwin's research was carried out on the Galapagos Islands in the Pacific Ocean. They were an excellent place to research how species develop, as they were extremely remote from human interference. You could find out about his work on finches, by using the Internet or library.

1859 saw the publication of *On the Origin of Species by Means of Natural Selection*, causing a storm of controversy. In *Origins*, Darwin outlined his theory of evolution, which radically challenged the creationist paradigm generally accepted at the time.

Darwin initially accepted the creationist paradigm, which has the Bible as its basis, and studied to become a Church of England priest. His studies on the voyage of the Beagle led him to challenge this paradigm. What he observed as a scientist made him question what was, at that point, a generally held truth and propose a new paradigm – that life had evolved through natural selection. This is sometimes known as Darwinism.

When it was first proposed, his theory caused outrage, but by the end of the 19th Century it had been accepted by virtually everyone. This is an example of paradigm shift – the underpinning beliefs being challenged and changed and then everyone getting on with the new paradigm. Most Christian groups incorporated it into their belief structure fairly quickly, arguing that evolution is part of the will of God.

GURU TV

Watch the Science and Technology programme, for more influencial people in science, in a journey through the major advances in medicine during the 20th Century.

In January 2001, an oil tanker, the Jessica, foundered off the Galapagos Islands. The oil spill caused a severe threat to the unique plants and animal species, which Darwin studied while researching his theory of evolution.

Science and technology

Research focus

Darwin was an influential scientist who changed the way in which we view the world. Other scientists you should know a little about might include:

Galileo Galilei (1564–1642)
Isaac Newton (1642–1727)
Joseph Priestly (1733–1804)
Michael Faraday (1791–1867)
Dimitri Mendeleev (1834–1907)
Albert Einstein (1879–1955)
Francis Watson (1928–) and James Crick (1916–)
Stephen Hawking (1942–)

How many scientists are important enough for you to need to know about? Try and get to know the basics and, if you're interested, delve a little bit deeper. The Internet is a useful source of biographical information.

All the important scientists haven't been men. Try looking up Marie Curie (1867–1934), Rosalind Franklin (1920–58), Lise Meitner (1878–1968) or Maria Goeppert-Mayer (1906–1972).

KEY SKILLS

These scientists could be the subject of a simple IT search, using the Internet or a CD ROM, for Key Skill IT3.1

KEY SKILLS IT3.1

Climate change

Scientists who study the Earth's atmosphere believe that human activity has caused changes to occur in its chemical composition. This could cause long-term damage to the Earth's ecosystem. In General Studies, you are likely to be asked to explain what changes are occurring and why scientists think they could cause problems.

How is the climate changing?

There are lots of climate changes you need to have at least a basic understanding about. You'll probably have heard of them all – but what exactly do they mean?

GURU WEBSITE

Find out more about all kinds of climate change on the BBC AS Guru™ website.

The greenhouse effect	This is the heating up of the atmosphere due to 'greenhouse gases' and is one most people get confused about.
Acid rain	This is where chemicals (Sulphur Dioxide – SO_2 and Nitrogen Oxides – NO in various forms) emitted by burning fossil fuels cause rainwater to become more acidic. This affects plant and animal life. In high concentrations, entire ecosystems can be harmed. The chemicals are moved by winds and concentrate in particular areas – British acid rain often lands in Scandinavia.
Damage to the ozone layer	The ozone layer is a layer of gases in the upper atmosphere which filter out ultraviolet (UV) rays from the sun. Too much UV light can cause increased skin cancers and damage vegetation. Chlorofluorocarbons (CFCs) present in aerosol propellant and refrigeration systems, break down the layer, allowing more UV to reach the Earth. There have been efforts to remove CFCs from aerosols and other products, but they stay in the atmosphere for up to 100 years, so the problem continues.

The different types of climate change are linked, but they are essentially separate issues. You need to sort out the differences as this is one area that often gets confused, especially the the greenhouse effect and damage to the ozone layer.

The greenhouse effect

GURU TIP

The main greenhouse gas is carbon dioxide. It is responsible for over 70% of the greenhouse effect. Increasing CO_2 comes from burning fossil fuels because they contain carbon.

Coal, oil and gas are the fossilised remains of animal or plant life. All animals and plants contain carbon.

The greenhouse effect is an entirely natural process. greenhouse gases (such as carbon dioxide and water vapour) present in the Earth's atmosphere trap heat, which would otherwise be lost back to space. Without it, scientists believe the Earth would be around 15°C cooler – far too cold for human life to have evolved.

Human activity seems to have increased the amount of atmospheric greenhouse gases. More heat is trapped by the gases and scientists believe the average global temperature will increase. Otherwise known as the enhanced greenhouse effect, this could lead to global warming.

Figure show that global temperatures have increased by about 0.6°C over the last 120 years. It's not a steady rise, although the trend since about 1980 has been mainly upwards, at a rapid rate. Is this evidence to support global warming?.

Research focus
- Pressure groups, such as Greenpeace and Friends of the Earth
- The Department of the Environment, Transport and Regions (DETR)
- The Met Office (responsible for meteoroligical research)
- Climate research centres, such as at the University of East Anglia, Norwich.

Evidence for global warming

- The concentrations of greenhouse gases in the atmosphere have increased, in Europe since the Industrial Revolution. This is probably due to burning fossil fuels.

- Global average temperatures have increased by about half a degree, since accurate records began in the 19th Century.

- Increasing CO_2 **emissions** is changing the composition of the atmosphere. This will cause a warming effect.

Evidence against global warming?

- Global temperatures fluctuate naturally. Fossil records and tree rings show variations of 3°C occurred, before people started to add more CO_2 to the atmosphere. It could be a natural fluctuation.

- Natural feedback systems may mean that increases in greenhouse gases won't result in in global warming. For example, plankton absorb CO_2 from the atmosphere, so more CO_2 may simply mean more plankton.

> Plankton are primary producers that live in oceans and use CO_2 in the same way as plants: by absorbing it from the atmosphere to use for photosynthesis.

KEY SKILLS
IT3

Impacts of global warming in Britain

There is much debate over how Britain could be affected by global warming. Many scientists disagree and the truth is that no-one really knows for sure:

- temperatures may rise by as much as 3°C but impacts are uncertain
- it's possible that warm ocean currents, such as the Gulf Stream, moving towards Britain would be reversed, leading to cooling
- rainfall levels may change as well – some places could become wetter, leading to flooding; some could get drier, causing droughts
- severe storms could be more common due to higher levels of atmospheric energy
- crops grown could change – Mediterranean varieties may be grown, further north
- a Mediterranean climate could also bring pests and diseases with it
- sea levels could rise by 70cm by 2050. Coastal areas could be in danger from increased flooding and erosion – particularly low-lying areas such as East Anglia. Industries and nuclear power stations on the coast could be in particular danger.

However life in Britain changes, there are bound to be other nations more severely affected. Places like Bangladesh and the Maldives are extremely low-lying and already suffer major flood disasters. They are also relatively poor and less able to put anti-flooding measures into force and provide help when flooding occurs. In Britain, we have the resources to deal with the problems global warming may bring.

KEY SKILLS
Global warming would make a good issue to research for IT3 project

> Science and technology

You might be provided with cartoons to use in an exam – they are a good source of interesting information. They do need to be used with care though, as sometimes the meaning isn't as clear as you'd like – the humour often hides the message. This cartoon shows how the issue of greenhouse gas emissions are often misunderstood. It shows people from eicher countries are reluctant to change the way they live their lives in order to be greener.

"But greenhouse gases are my only pleasure in life"

GURU TIP
Try to keep up-to-date with what scientists think will happen if global warming gets worse.
Use newspapers, magazines, such as New Scientist (they have an excellent web site) and TV news.

Natural hazards

Hurricanes, volcanoes, earthquakes and floods are all natural hazards – natural events that have an impact on people and their property. They are a fact of life, the wild side of nature that people have little or no control over.

In this section you'll be looking at one hazard – hurricanes – to show how science and technology have tried to tame the forces of nature. Scientists are aiming to help people cope more easily with natural processes by finding ways to control them. You can use this example as a starting point to illustrate whether science has been successful at controlling nature, or not, and what other factors play a part.

The hurricane hazard

Hurricanes are tropical storms with winds in excess of 118km/hr. They are called hurricanes in the Americas, and in Asia they are known as cyclones or typhoons. The effects are the same – warm oceans produce storms that batter coastal areas and then die out as they pass inland and their supply of warm water disappears.

The large storms that hit Britain aren't hurricanes. They can have gusts of the same force, but hurricanes are tropical storms with tight, spiral winds. The 'Great Storm' of 1987, in southern Britain, had sustained winds of 100km/hr. Hurricane winds can reach more than twice this velocity.

When hurricanes hit land, their winds damage or destroy buildings, crops and services, such as electricity supplies. Large waves and extreme rainfall cause flooding and landslides. Lives are badly affected and many deaths can occur if people can't get out of the hurricane's path.

People who live in hurricane-prone areas can prepare for storms because they occur in the same areas, year after year. There are many ways in which technology can be used to help people prepare and to minimise the impacts of hurricanes.

Technology and hurricanes

Despite extensive research, there is currently no way to prevent hurricanes. US researchers proposed detonating nuclear bombs in the core of developing storms in an attempt to disrupt their energy levels – radioactivity problems mean that this has never been tried! Some researchers believe that human activity might be making hurricanes stronger and more frequent. Global warming seems to be increasing the amount of heat energy in the atmosphere and this could mean that large storms and hurricanes have more of the energy they need to develop. If the Earth is getting warmer then we may start getting hurricanes in other areas of the world as well.

Predicting hurricanes

Hurricanes are difficult to predict, often moving unexpectedly and getting stronger or weaker for unexplained reasons. Satellite images can be used to identify potential hurricanes at an early stage and monitor their development and movement. This form of long-term warning allows scientists to monitor storms carefully. Without satellite images, some hurricanes might still take everyone by surprise and there would certainly be less warning. These are a great example of how technology has helped – satellite images have only been used in the last 30 years.

GURU TIP
The important thing to think about in this chapter is how people's lives can be improved by science and technology. This is what you'd need to discuss in a AS General Studies exam.

GURU TIP
Try to get an idea of the impacts of hurricanes by looking at Internet images or TV coverage.
The sheer force could blow you away!

See page 61, for more information on global warming.

Hurricanes don't actually move very fast – usually at less than 50km/hr. Their winds circulate very quickly around the centre, which is where the damage occurs. Because they are fairly slow-moving, they can be monitored and warnings can be provided to reduce damage to property and loss of lives.

Long-range reconnaissance aircraft can fly over hurricanes and provide accurate measurements of air pressure and wind speed using special equipment. These allow a much more accurate prediction of the likely force of a hurricane. Aircraft are a good example of technology. Long-range aircraft that are capable of flying through hurricanes are an even better example!

Aircraft don't usually need to be strengthened to fly though a hurricane – although they could get blown off course.

Rainfall radar can be used close to land to get a more accurate picture of how hurricanes are developing and where they are likely to end up. Radar works over a shorter range than satellite imaging, but it is still useful.

Preparing for hurricanes

Scientific monitoring means that we are better at understanding how hurricanes develop and why they form. Increased understanding means that we can do more to reduce their impacts – and that understanding is all down to technology.

- Advanced technology allows hurricane shelters to be built and for buildings to be strengthened. Hurricane shelters are often underground and made from reinforced concrete to ensure they survive winds of up to 250km/hr. Individual buildings can be fitted with storm-proof shutters and can be strengthened. Reinforced sea walls and flood barriers mean that coastal flooding can be reduced as well. Better building technology means that we can survive better, physically, when hurricanes hit.
- If hurricanes can be predicted then people need to be warned. There's no point making a prediction if you don't tell anyone about it! This is also where technology comes in handy. Radio and TV are excellent ways of warning lots of people very quickly. Up to the minute information can also be found on the Internet to inform people how storms are progressing. With accurate and up to date information, people can make their own choices about what to do – evacuate, sit tight or go to a shelter. How would people evacuate? Planes, trains and automobiles are all modern inventions that allow people to get away from hurricanes quickly.
- Technology allows lots of people to be educated about hurricanes very quickly and efficiently. The media and Internet are useful here as well. In Bermuda grocery bags are printed with information about what to do if a hurricane is forecast – a great example of how mass printing technology getting a message across to lots of people.

Technology can also help after a hurricane. Helicopters can bring in food supplies, rescue people from flooded areas and airlift casualties to well-equipped hospitals with access to modern medical technology. Disease can be avoided by purifying water or using bottled water. News and information can quickly be broadcast to let people know what to do. All of this is technology in action.

If you have access to the Internet take a look at some of the sites providing hurricane education. Start by typing 'hurricane' as the keyword in a search engine. You can find out how to make your house hurricane-proof! There are even books for younger children to help explain about hurricanes.

GURU TIP
It's worth finding out about other natural hazards. Geography teachers are a good source of information. and Geography textbooks often have maps indicating where hurricanes and other hazards occur.

Science and technology

KEY SKILLS
Researching a hurricane, such as Georges, on the web should allow you to collect enough information to produce a short report to satisfy Key Skill IT3.3.

See page 6 for more information about what is required for each Key Skill.

KEY SKILLS
IT 3.3

Natural hazards: a case study

Research focus: hurricanes

Good places to find out about hurricanes include:

- newspapers and television news will have up-to-date examples
- the Met Office, which you can find it on the Internet at www.metoffice.gov.uk/
- centres, such as the US National Oceanic and Atmospheric Administration, which you can find at www.noaa.gov
- newspapers from places affected by Hurricanes. USA Today has a section on its website at www.usatoday.com/weather/hurricane/whur0.htm that is excellent.

Does all this technology actually make a difference? Has science allowed people to tame hurricanes or at least to save lives? The best way to find out is to look at a hurricane case study. You can then use an example to provide evidence that technology has or hasn't been successful in making the world a safer place. You won't have to know detailed examples or even talk about natural hazards, necessarily – this is all about the role technology has to play in the modern world.

Case study: Hurricane Georges

Hurricane Georges formed in September 1998, tracking through the eastern Caribbean before passing over the tip of Florida and through the Gulf of Mexico to Louisiana. It affected relatively poor Caribbean countries and the USA, allowing the use of technology to be assessed. The US is a much richer country and has much more access to the types of technology discussed in this chapter. Caribbean countries are much poorer in comparison, so aren't able to do as many things as the US, as they can't afford the technology, either as countries, or as individuals.

Map indicating the path of Hurricane Georges

Hurricanes are given names. In the Caribbean they use alternate male and female names, but before 1979 only women's names were used! Georges is pronounced with a French accent.

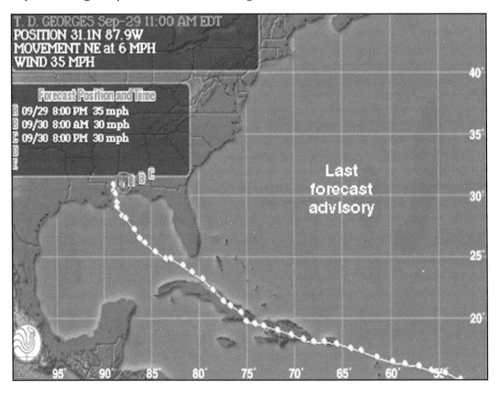

Source: National Hurricane Center and Weather Services Corp

COUNTRY AFFECTED	PEOPLE EVACUATED	DEATHS	DAMAGE TO PROPERTY
USA	3 million	4	estimated $4–5b insurance damage major power cuts
Cuba	200 000	5	20 000 homes flooded crop damage
Haiti		240	flooding in capital city major building damage
Dominican Republic		283	10 000 homeless 90% plantations destroyed $111m damage to power grid damage estimated at $1b
Puerto Rico		21	28 000 homeless 80% population without water damage estimated at $2b
St Kitts-Nevis		5	3000 homeless 85% buildings damaged damage estimated at $402b
Antigua and Barbuda		2	major building damage power cuts

GURU TIP
You could use an atlas to find out more about these countries and their relative wealths.

GURU TIP
Remember that your focus has to be on technology and how it can be used.

Science and technology

What can Hurricane Georges tell us about the use of technology?

Hurricane Georges was a major hazard but it seems to have affected different countries in different ways. Very few people died in the USA, although the financial costs of the hazard were much higher. In Haiti, many more people died but there was less financial loss. Better technology in the US seems to have helped reduce casualties by protecting people and providing more accurate warnings, which were communicated quickly and efficiently, enabling nearly 3 million people to evacuate their homes. The financial losses were higher, but many were covered by insurance companies. The United States is much wealthier, so $4–5 billion is a less significant loss than $402 million is to St Kitt's and Nevis.

The Dominican Republic demonstrates the problems less economically developed countries (LEDCs) may have. Inaccurate predictions and poor communications made problems worse rather than better. Impacts, such as flooding, can't be dealt with as easily and shelters and buildings were not as strong as in the other countries hit by the hurricane. The technology is not as developed. As a result, more people died.

The problem of countries, such as the Dominican Republic, can be exacerbated by natural hazards, such as Hurricane Georges. Cash crops, which provide crucial income, where destroyed, damaging the country in the long-term. As a result, it is less able to afford technology to reduce the impact of future hazards – a vicious circle.

It seems clear that rich countries have better protection than poorer ones, as they can afford better technology. However, even in the US, people died. Perhaps technology can't tame nature but it can help cushion us from some of its effects if people can afford it in the first place.

Research focus

Think about other areas where technology has improved people's life. You could start with areas, such as:

- crop production
- media and communications
- medical science
- transport safety.

Energy: fuels

In General Studies you'll need to know where energy comes from and about the impacts of its production and use. You'll need to be able to talk about alternative sources and what should happen in the future.

KEY SKILLS
Analysing the graphs and tables on this page would fulfil Key Skill N3.1

Energy in Britain – using graphs and tables

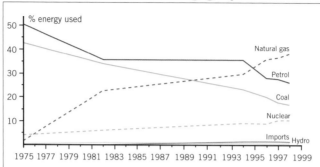

Developed countries, such as Britain use a lot of energy. This country relies mainly on fossil fuels but this brings pollution problems. Look at this graph, which shows the sources of energy used in Britain from 1975 to 1998.

In General Studies you can expect to be given graphs and tables to interpret. Below you can see some of the sorts of things you might be asked when looking at the graph on the left and some of the points you could draw from it.

> **Focus questions:** describe the trends shown by the graph.
> What are the advantages/disadvantages of this kind of graph for showing this data?
> Calculate the percentage of Britain's energy needs met by fossil fuels in 1998.
> Compare the figures for 1975 with those for 1998.
> Suggest reasons for the changes in energy fuel use between 1975 and 1998.

KEY SKILLS N3.1

- coal has declined steadily in importance from about 43% in 1975 to 19% in 1998
- oil declined between 1975 and 1982 from 50% to 36%. Since then oil has stayed at about 33-36% of energy use
- gas has increased dramatically from 2% in 1975 to 38% in 1998
- nuclear power has increased slightly but is much less important than fossil fuels
- alternatives and energy imports are fairly insignificant at about 1% of use

Any way of presenting data has advantages and disadvantages. For example:

Advantages: The energy graph above presents the information as percentages of total energy use for each fuel, sp you can see how gas has grown in popularity as a fuel and how coal has declined. The balance between fuel types over time can be shown. Percentages are a clear way to compare figures.

Disadvantages: You don't see the overall increase in energy use between 1975 and 1998. Using percentages masks the fact that the use of nuclear power, for example, has increased from 8.1mtoe to 23mtoe — nearly three times. You have to work out the percentage of use from oil in 1975 first.

This table shows the growth of total energy use in Britain over the same period.

1975	1982	1994	1996	1997	1998	
171.9	196.5	216.9	230.6	225.3	228.5	figures in mtoe

Notice the overall rise in energy use. You might need to describe the trend or to draw a line graph to show the increase. There was a steady growth between 1975 and 1994 and a rapid jump between 1994 and 1996 Since then the use has decreased slightly.

mtoe stands for million tonnes of oil equivalent. This is the standard way to measure fuel use - it's just the amount of energy equivalent to burning a million tonnes of oil.

Consequences of fuel use

Below you can see a summary of the different fuels used in the UK and their consequences. Use it as a starting point for discussion about the pros and cons of different fuel types. This kind of question could easily come up in an exam.

Coal:
– mainly used for electricity generation
– less use as a home fuel as electricity or gas are cleaner and easier to use
– major environmental consequences – especially acid rain/greenhouse gases
– decrease in use since 1982 due to closure of UK mines from 1985 following the miners' strike
– large reserves, both in UK and elsewhere

Oil:
– main use in transport (as petrol/diesel); also heating and making electricity
– drop in use, possibly due to more efficient vehicle engines
– major environmental consequences – acid rain, greenhouse gases, oil spills
– UK production has increased from 0.2 mtoe in 1970 to 150 mtoe in 1999
– adequate reserves, although ultimately supplies will run out

Gas:
– increasing use as domestic fuel (cooking and heating)
– in 1990s major increase in gas fired power stations producing electricity
– cleanest fossil fuel with less environmental consequences than coal or oil
– smallest reserves of all fossil fuels

Nuclear Power:
– used to generate electricity – over 25% of UK electricity production
– power stations are ageing – many being closed down
– cheap to produce but costs of closing/securing stations and waste are huge
– no major contribution to greenhouse gases or acid rain
– dangers of radioactive contamination or accident

Hydro-electric power
– created by falling water passing through dams
– minor fuel contributor nationally
– locally can be an important fuel for remote communities
– does have environmental consequences – dams can impact on aquatic ecosystems for example

Alternative energy sources

There are also alternative sources of power – wind, solar, wave power and so on. In Britain, these contribute about 3% of the electricity we use, (more than double the figure in 1992). Many people doubt that these can play a major role in energy production in Britain. What if you rely on wind turbines and the wind doesn't blow? You'd need hundreds of wind turbines to produce the same amount of electricity as a large power station. Where would they all go?

Supporters of alternative energy argue that since fossil fuels will eventually run out, non-polluting sources of energy must be sought. Electric cars are now used in some parts of the world and alternative energy is more viable as fossil fuel prices go up and research continues. In the long run, alternative energy may be the answer.

Issues for the energy future

- Fossil fuels are running out and become more expensive as stocks dwindle. They are also the heaviest pollutants.
- Nuclear energy can produce electricity but the long-term financial costs are huge. Potential environmental damage is great should an accident occur.
- Can alternatives produce enough power?
- How to deal with non-electricity requirements such as transport
- Do we use far too much energy? Could we reduce usage and be more efficient?

All the information here is for total energy use. That includes use for transport and industry. It's not the same thing as just electricity generation

KEY SKILLS
A presentation, using images to summarise the advantages and disadvantages of different fuels would make an excellent subject to achieve Key Skill C3.1b.

Science and technology

GURU TIP
It's a good idea to research more about sources of alternative power. Try contacting: the Department of Energy
Pressure groups
Greenpeace; Friends of the Earth
Power companies
British Gas, Powergen, National Power
Oil companies
Shell, BP, Texaco
Alternative power companies
Scottish Hydro, National Wind Power, Intersolar.

Energy: the nuclear debate

If you don't already have a point of view about nuclear power it's the sort of issue you need to have an opinion about for General Studies. If you do have an established point of view, it's important that you are able to balance your opinions and understand opinions which might oppose your own. You need to be able to put forward both sides of the argument to score highly in an exam.

Is nuclear power the answer to all our energy problems or a dangerous and unnecessary scientific risk?

Is the risk of an accident worth the gains from energy supply?

Is the nuclear industry too secretive or is opposition just scare-mongering without any basis in fact?

How a nuclear power station works

In many respects, nuclear power stations are just like most power stations. They boil water to turn turbines, which produce electricity through a generator. It's just the fuel they use which makes them different. The exceptions to this are alternative sources of energy, such as wind and water power, where the energy source turns the turbine directly and no water needs to be boiled.

Conventional power stations most commonly use fossil fuels (coal, oil, gas) to heat water. Nuclear power stations use Uranium fuel rods. Uranium is a naturally-occurring material with an important property: its atoms occasionally split into two equal portions. This process releases energy, as well as two or three neutrons from the atom. These neutrons then collide with other atoms, causing them to split, too, and continuing the reaction. In nuclear power stations, this reaction is controlled and can be made continuous – it carries on and on and can be used to harness useful amounts of energy in the form of heat. It's this heat that boils the water.

Uranium has several isotopes. Isotopes are variants of the same element. The number of neutrons in the atom varies, so each isotope has subtle differences. The most-used isotope of Uranium is U_{235}. It's not important that you know this, but it's always good to add a few specific facts, if you can, to show a more detailed knowledge of the subject.

Advantages of nuclear power

On the other side of the argument, nuclear power does have several advantages over other forms of power generation.

- It is a fuel which could go on producing electricity for many years into the future, as very small amounts of Uranium are actually used. It also contributes far fewer greenhouse gases to the atmosphere than fossil fuels.

- Radioactivity is released in small quantities from nuclear power stations. However, radiation is also present in the natural environment, in low 'background' levels and in X-rays, luminous watches and fluorescent lights. Mostly, nuclear power stations make very small contributions to this background level – the nuclear industry claims they are almost insignificant. Granite rocks in Cornwall release more radioactivity into the environment than most nuclear power stations.

- There is radioactive material naturally occurring all around you because Uranium and other radioactive materials are found in low concentrations throughout the earth. Granite happens to have a higher concentration of this type of material, so gives off more radiation.

KEY SKILLS

Should more nuclear power stations be built in the UK?

This would make a great subject for a discussion and provide evidence for Key Skill C3.1a.

GURU TIP

In the end, people will always disagree over an issue like nuclear power. There isn't a right or wrong answer. It's all about opinions.

Radiation hasn't always been thought of as dangerous. In fact radioactive tonic water was sold during the 1920s as a health cure!

Problems with nuclear fuel

As you'll probably have heard, there are some downsides to the production of nuclear power. Here are some of the issues that worry people:

- The process of splitting atoms for power is similar to the reaction that takes place in a nuclear bomb, but the aim in a reactor is to make a continuous flow of energy, whereas a bomb aims to create as much energy as possible at one time. Pro-nuclear supporters counteract this by saying that by controlling the amount of Uranium present, it is possible to ensure that nuclear power stations can't explode.

- Another side-product of the nuclear power industry is that radioactive material is produced. Radioactive material continues to emit radiation over a long period of time. Radiation is dangerous to human health as it can damage cells within the body, which then form the basis for cancerous growths.

  Large emissions of radiation can cause significant damage to the biosphere and human health. Cancers, such as leukaemia, can develop, and radioactive material can enter the food chain if crops or animals are exposed.

  After the Chernobyl nuclear incident (see below), sheep in Wales were exposed to the effects of a radiation cloud which travelled from the Ukraine over Britain. The slaughter of sheep from this area was controlled for years afterwards to make sure no contaminated meat got into the human food chain, despite the incident happening hundreds of miles away.

Nuclear accidents

There have been a number of nuclear incidents over the years, both in Britain and abroad although, in general, these have been due to human error rather than problems with the nuclear technology itself.

Famous nuclear incidents include:
Chernobyl (Ukraine, 1986) – Probably the most infamous nuclear incident. Engineers wanted to test automatic safety procedures and disconnected cooling pumps from the reactor core in order to carry out an experiment. The reactor started to overheat and steam built up until the heat became uncontrollable and a massive explosion blew the roof off the reactor unit, causing a huge release of radiation.

Three Mile Island (USA, 1979) – Two coolant pumps failed, a valve stuck and the reactor overheated, leading to a build up of hydrogen inside the reactor unit. The reactor was eventually controlled and only a small amount of radioactive material was released. For a time, the station was in danger of releasing large amounts of radioactive material.

There have also been examples of lower-level releases of radiation into the sea or atmosphere, and of workers being effected. In Britain, this has occurred at Sellafield in Cumbria and at Dounreay in northern Scotland.

In nuclear accidents, such as at Chernobyl, no nuclear 'explosion' actually occurred. Explosions in these cases are usually due to the build up of pressure within the secure reactor core, and not to the actual nuclear reaction.

The nuclear industry is very safety-conscious and aware of the need to reassure the public that the industry is safe.

The biosphere is just the whole natural environment – the air, earth, plants, animals and humans. It's a good word to use to talk about the environment.

Another detail you could use to impress examiners is that the radioactive material in granite is called radon and some people in Cornwall were considering suing the Government for allowing houses to be built on granite containing so much radiation that they felt their health would be at risk.

Have a look at the points of view on p67, for more arguments to use in a debate about nuclear power.

Science and technology

Energy: Sizewell and the future

Britain's most modern nuclear power station, Sizewell B, is located on the Suffolk coast near the small town of Leiston, which has a population 5500. It is next to the older Sizewell A reactor. The reactor was opened in 1995 and produces 1188 MW of electricity. Current government policy is that no more nuclear power stations should be built – they are too expensive to shut down and make safe when they become old and are no longer wanted. But consider questions like these ones below.

> Think about how much energy you use in the course of a day. Think of all the ways you've used energy since you got up this morning – from the first cuppa to the last time you switched a light on.
>
> What happens when fossil fuels run low?
>
> Can people cope in today's world without supplies of electricity?
>
> What alternatives are there?

GURU TIP

Try to work out why two nuclear power stations have been built at Sizewell. You could use websites to get a detailed map to look at geographical reasons for choosing the site. Try www.multimap.com as a starting point.

Sizewell B is the UK's only pressurised water reactor (PWR), see page 64 for details on how it works. These are common in the USA. Three Mile Island is an early version of a PWR (see page 69). After looking at the different views on page 71, try and consider what type of person might express each of these views? Beware of sterotyping people. In this case it was a school secretary who thought another power station should be built and a retired engineer who was strongly opposed to it. It's important to take a range ofopinions and make sense of them, quickly and efficiently.

These are questions that you may be asked to consider in General Studies. On the page opposite, you will see comments from people who actually live near a nuclear power station. Read them and use them as the basis for a debate, or as a starting point for finding out more about the arguments on both sides of the debate.

Research the nuclear debate

Useful places to start searching for further information on the nuclear debate include:

* The Department of Energy
* Department of the Environment, Transport and Regions
* British Energy (who own most UK nuclear power stations)
* The Green Party
* Non-Governmental pressure groups such as Greenpeace
* Local anti-nuclear groups

> **Research Focus**
>
> You could research a famous nuclear incident or 'leaks' that have occurred in Britain. Most nuclear stations have visitors centres which will tell you a lot more about the nuclear industry – but beware of bias! You could compare Britain's nuclear policy with another country – perhaps France, which has a lot more nuclear stations.

Local opinions on Sizewell B

The people who live in the area surrounding Sizewell have strong views about nuclear power. It's perhaps surprising that more people who live close to nuclear stations seem to be in favour of them than people who live further away. Can you think why?

> The safety record of the British nuclear industry is excellent. In general we have a record to be proud of, and the stations at Sizewell are no exception to that.

> Fossil fuels are going to run out and we have to find alternatives if we are going to maintain our quality of life. I understand about nuclear waste and the fear of accidents, but I'm sure that with time we can find a safe way of storing waste and we know that the safety systems at nuclear plants have to be second to none.

> The environmental damage created by Sizewell is massive. To start with it's an aesthetic nightmare along one of the most beautiful stretches of coastline in East Anglia. It's Heritage Coast you know. The potential for a major incident worries me greatly.

> The traffic that passes through the village is tremendous and people don't slow down. It's all down to the power station.

> Without Sizewell there really would be no major employer. Local businesses would lose so much trade as well. Without the stations Leiston would simply die.

> During the building phase workers were attracted from all over the country. By no means all the jobs went to local people. There aren't that many long term jobs either.

> Economically nuclear power is a joke right now. The running costs are small I'll accept. You don't need much fuel and the workforce isn't huge really. The building costs are more expensive, especially with all the safety systems they need, but it's the decommissioning costs that need to be fully taken into account. This is the cost of closing down the stations and making them and their fuel safe. There are all sorts of long term safety risks associated with waste and decommissioned stations.

> For me it's a matter of where we get our energy from in the long term. What other solution is there that we can be sure of? I accept that we can try and reduce our use of energy, but even so we'll still need fuel sources we can trust. To me that's nuclear power.

> One thing that really annoys me about nuclear power is that its backers always argue that alternative energy could never make up the gap that we'd need if we closed out nuclear stations down. Well, it wouldn't do would it? If you look at how much money has been thrown into nuclear research over the past fifty years and compare that with the minuscule amounts used to research alternatives you can figure out why. Give alternatives the same resources and we'd see a much bigger contribution being made.

KEY SKILLS
These opinions could form the starting point for a group role play, which could provide evidence for Key Skill C3.1a.

Science and technology

GURU TIP
With issues like nuclear power, you need to think about the economic, social, political and environmental issues. Try producing a table to show the pros and cons of Sizewell B, for the local area.

Sustainability & Agenda 21

GURU TIP

You could usefully find out about sustainable development projects in less economically developed countries (LEDCs) how they differ from non-sustainable projects. Geography teachers and textbooks are good sources.

Science and technology has brought many improvements – comfortable houses, means to travel quickly, energy, and much better medical technology. In 1911, life expectancy in the UK was 50–55 years; by 1995 it had improved to 75–80 years.

Science and technology can also damage the biosphere and create major problems for humans, for example global warming, the destruction of forests with their ecosystems, and the extinction of huge numbers of plant and animal species.

In June 1992, more than 178 governments attended the UN Conference on Environment and Development, held in Rio de Janiero, Brazil. The Rio summit was the first high-profile political summit focussing on the environment. Since then, there have been further meetings, at Kyoto in 1997 and The Hague in 2000.

You need to be able to evaluate the benefits and problems that scientific progress causes. These pages focus on sustainable development and its application through Agenda 21 and how they may be the solution to our global environmental problems.

Agenda 21

Agenda 21 was an action plan for **sustainable development** for the world into the 21st Century. It was drawn up at the 1992 Earth Summit in Rio de Janeiro. Sustainable development has been described in many ways but it has been hard to find a definition that satisfies everyone. Some suggestions are:

> Meeting the needs of the present without compromising the ability of future generations to meet their needs. (Brundtland Commission, 1987)
>
> Development which improves people's quality of life, within the carrying capacity of the Earth's life support systems. (United Nations Environment Programme)
>
> Note: carrying capacity is how much damage an ecosystem can take before it starts to be under serious threat.

KEY SKILLS

Agenda 21 is often misunderstood. A questionnaire could allow you to judge public opinion. The results would be a fascinating focus for a level 3 Application of Number project, if you develop some statistics.

These mean that sustainable development should work to improve people's lives today without destroying the natural environment or too many resources which future generations might need. The concept applies to development projects in Less Economically Developed Countries and to further development in the richer world.

What does Agenda 21 do?

Agenda 21 is about local people all over the world acting for sustainable development – it coined the phrase 'think global, act local'. It is 'a guide for individuals, businesses and governments' and covers a range of topics, from poverty to deforestation; health to waste management. Here are just two local projects under Agenda 21 in the UK.

- Plymouth Young Persons Agenda 21
  A project to encourage young people to express their opinions in the local decision-making process. It involved students, aged 3–15, across schools in Plymouth, building enthusiasm for environmental and political issues.
- Newcastle Schools Recycling Project
  Provided recycling facilities on local sites, to dispose of school and domestic waste responsibly. An educational element was developed for use in classrooms.

Both of these schemes use technology. The Plymouth schemes relies upon communications technology to get its message across; the Newcastle scheme depends on it to recycle material effectively. Both are small-scale, local schemes by local people – many experts say this is the best form of sustainable development.

KEY SKILLS
N3

What about global issues?

This article led the front page of the Observer on Sunday 26th November, 2000. The international climate conference in The Hague collapsed when countries failed to agree on a set of international rules for controlling emissions of carbon dioxide (CO_2). European countries wanted to ensure the USA made serious cuts to its emissions of CO_2. The USA wanted to use carbon sinks and the process of 'trading emissions', which are discussed below.

Carbon sinks

Carbon sinks are anything which absorbs large amounts of carbon from the atmosphere. Plankton in oceans do this, but the best-known carbon sinks are forests. The USA proposed planting trees to soak up CO_2 instead of cutting CO_2 emissions – the trees recycle the CO_2 into oxygen. However, scientists are unsure how effective this would be.

Trading emissions

Trading emissions means that a rich country pays poorer countries not to burn fossil fuels. The rich country can then carry on its production of fossil fuels as it has 'traded' away its CO_2 to another nation. Environmentalists argue that this fails to cut emissions globally and also helps to maintain the division between rich and poor countries – something that sustainable development seeks to reduce.

Do science and technology have energy solutions?

Potential solutions do exist, but they may not be fully developed yet, or they cost more money than simply to keep on burning fossil fuels. Solutions include:

- energy efficiency – reducing the amount of energy required by using insulation, double glazing or cars with smaller, less polluting engines

- alternative fuels – use something other than fossil fuels (see page 63).

- electric cars – the electricity still has to come from somewhere, though

- use less energy – but this means altering our lifestyle. Could we do this?

- make energy more expensive – but look at the protests when taxes on petrol are perceived to make it more expensive than in Europe.

> **Climate Talks End in Disarray**
>
> Global talks aimed at saving the world from climatic mayhem collapsed in chaos yesterday, dealing a potentially fatal blow to efforts to cut industrial gases which threaten the planet"

> **GURU TIP**
> Check the section on climate change to make sure you understand what types of gases might be involved and how they might threaten the planet.

> **GURU TIP**
> Look for as many different impacts of industrial growth as you can. Try starting with literature from pressure groups such as Friends of the Earth.

> **GURU TIP**
> Try to keep up-to-date with what scientists think will happen if global warming gets worse. Use newspapers, magazines, such as New Scientist (they have an excellent web site) and TV news.

Science and technology

Genetics and cloning

The genetic code

Human genetics and **cloning** are areas of biomedical science that are surrounded by major scientific and moral issues. Advances in both could allow scientists to cure major medical conditions and eliminate genetic disorders, such as cystic fibrosis. On the other hand, it could also lead to the spectre of designer babies and selective breeding of humans. You might have come across these issues at GCSE level, in Science or RE, and are they ones you need to be aware of for General Studies.

In 1953, James Watson and Francis Crick (Cambridge University) unravelled the structure of deoxyribosenucleic acid, more commonly known as DNA. DNA is a complex molecule found in all cell nuclei and is the blueprint for everything that happens in the human body, so it has been called the building block of life. This discovery has led to major developments in molecular biology. It's a good example of how scientists can take a new piece of understanding to develop specific ideas.

Human DNA is found in the form of **chromosomes**. A chromosome is a strand of DNA. In human cells there are 23 pairs of chromosomes. Each chromosome is split into regions – these regions are called **genes**. A pair of genes controls a specific feature, such as eye colour or gender. Genes are inherited from your parents – so if there's a problem with their genes you might also inherit it.

DNA fingerprinting

DNA is a huge, complex molecule made up of millions of simple units, called **bases**. The order of bases determines the genetic code and, therefore, everything from eye colour, to leaf shape and flower scent. This order, or sequence, is so highly specific, that the chance of two individuals of the same species having the same code is considered to be virtually impossible. Scientists developed DNA fingerprinting to break down a sample of DNA into the component bases, to produce a comparable pattern. This is useful in forensic assessment, as at a crime scene a piece of hair, blood, skin or semen, can be sampled and used to compare with suspects' DNA.

Genetic disorders

An example of this is colour blindness – a disorder caused by a gene mutation that mainly affects males. You might want to research cystic fibrosis and haemophilia.

Manipulating genes – what does it mean?

Genetic engineering

The process of manipulating the genetic code directly. By introducing, mutating or deleting a specific sequence of DNA, a particular characteristic can be aquired, altered or removed from an organism. By changing the genetic code, the characteristic should be passed onto offspring.

Gene therapy

This is a technique that implants a fully functional gene into an individual with a defective gene in order to compensate for it. There have been attempts to use this approach to help people with cystic fibrosis.

Xenotransplantation

This is a method of transplanting organs or tissue between different species – 'xeno' means foreign. Pig organs have been used as short-term replacements for human organs within the last few years.

GURU TIP

It's worth knowing more about Watson and Crick. Find out about their research and how they developed ideas, using other people's work. This would make a good example of how scientific methods progress.

What is the Human Genome Project?

The US National Institutes of Health and the Department of Energy started this project in the 1980s, to determine the base sequence of the human **genome**. This is a mammoth experiment that has become a global collaboration. The entire genome is due to be sequenced in 2003, a project spanning two decades and costing over $3 billion and this won't even tell us what all the genes do!

The Human Genome Project is attempting to **map** out the DNA structure of humans. Mapping them will make it possible to identify all the genes in the body.

Mapping genomes is not new. Already, scientists have sequenced the genomes of species of a worm, yeast and the fruit fly; all relatively simple organisms. The Human Genome Project leads to the possibility of being able to research how individual genes work and how they contribute to diseases and genetic conditions. Ultimately, treatments and drugs could be developed.

The research is being carried out by a number of different groups. The public project includes research done by The Wellcome Trust and the Sanger Centre. Other companies are carrying out private research. The private and public debate has led to controversy, as the public project immediately makes its data available on the Internet for interested parties to use. In order for the private companies to make back the money they have invested in the project, they may patent their sequenced genes (in order to prevent other companies from using the sequence) and allowing them to profit from any products made using the sequence.

Patenting this information allows companies to charge royalties if other researchers want to work on those genes. Technically, they could ban other people from working on those genes. So, who owns the genome? Does anyone have the right to patent part of the human genetic makeup? Is it fair to earn money from genetic research when the results could be so beneficial?

Ethical and moral challenges

The publication of the human genome map could lead to a new era in medical research but what are the issues surrounding the provision of all this information?

- Testing of unborn foetuses for genetic disorders is now possible. What if a test shows that a child is a carrier of a disorder, which means they could die before the age of 14? Should parents allow a child who will certainly die to be born?

- What if the test allows people to abort foetuses with cystic fibrosis? Who determines what the quality of life for a person with CF will be like? Should we not allow such a child to be born? If the option to abort is there, what does this say about our opinion on the quality of life of those who have the disease already?

- Should embryos which are predisposed to conditions, such as Huntingdon's Chorea or breast cancer, which occur later on in life, be considered in a different context to those with conditions which are evident at birth? Who decides that these people have a poorer quality of life than other people? Who has the right to play God?

- Should insurance companies be allowed to ask for genetic tests before providing life insurance? It would allow the insurance company to factor the risks more accurately when calculating premiums. Would you want your insurance company to charge you a higher premium, if you had a predisposition to a known genetic disorder? Would you want to pay a higher premium if you knew you didn't have a predisposition to a known genetic disorder?

KEY SKILLS
C3.2

KEY SKILLS

Further reading here would allow you to synthesis information for Key Skill C3.2.

Science and technology

GURU TIP

You could be asked to discuss the pros and cons of cloning or research into human genetics. These are major ethical issues that examiners love! Use newspapers, the Internet and popular science magazines, to get both sides of the story.

Cloning and research

Why does everyone seem to have something to say about cloning? This section looks into the implications of cloning and genetic research and acknowledges the different fears and concerns that all sides are currently voicing. This is a subject that is worth following in the newspapers, as new technologies and developments are happening all the time.

Current research

- Scientists believe there is a genetic predisposition to breast cancer. This means that some women may be more likely to develop cancers because of their genetic makeup. Research into breast cancer is highly proactive at the moment. One of the most high-profile aims is to identify women with a predisposition to breast cancer, at an earlier stage. This would allow monitoring or treatment to be targeted more precisely and the treatment to be more specific and, therefore, more likely to succeed.
- Researchers have discovered a specific gene, which is over-active in patients with leukaemia. They are trialling specially developed immune cells, which can destory the cells with overactive genes, whilst ignoring healthy cells. This could lead to treatments for other types of cancer.
- Andi, the genetically modified monkey, was created in 2000. Genetic research using monkeys might allow scientists to study the mechanisms of complex brain diseases, such as Alzheimer's disease.

Cloning

Cloning is a procedure used to isolate a particular gene or set of genes and implant them into an organism, such as bacteria, so that the bacteria will reproduce the information.

Cloning is the way in which genetically identical offspring can be produced. In plants, cloning has been in operation for many years. The first experiment carried out involved the cloning of carrots – a cell was taken from a carrot and grown in a suitable medium. The cells grow and divide. One cell was chosen and grown, and developed into an embryo, which then developed into a new plant. This technique means that lots of identical offspring can be produced. Cloning plants is now a major commercial process.

The first experiments into animal cloning were carried out in frogs. It was only in 1997 that the first mammal was cloned – Dolly the sheep opened up a whole new debate into the ethics of cloning. If a sheep can be cloned, why not a human?

Human cloning does not necessarily have to lead to the development of identical humans. In fact, most of the interest in the idea at present involves what's called therapeutic cloning. This is the creation of human embryos in laboratories in order to extract embryonic stem cells from them. Stem cells are capable of developing into any cell in the body and could be used to provide genetic material, which could be implanted back into people's bodies – to help cure heart problems or even produce entire organs for transplants.

Research focus

Try to find out a little more about Dolly the Sheep. This would make a good example of scientific advances.

Where do they stem from?

The initial research on stem cells was done on aborted foetuses and unwanted embryos from IVF treatment. In the future, embryos could be grown especially to produce such material.

It has been possible to grow stem cells since 1998 and they are not in themselves, cloned material. Cloning would, however, allow identical material to be produced. This could have major advantages. For example, a leukaemia patient could have the perfect match for a bone marrow transplant produced by cloning, using the patients own skin cells, perhaps.

Arguments to support the development of human cloning include:

* reversing the ageing process
* eliminating heart attacks by cloning healthy heart cells which can then be injected into damaged areas
* growing embryonic stem cells to produce organs or tissues to repair or replace damaged ones: by producing skin for burn victims, brain cells for the brain damaged, for example
* reducing infertility
* cloning is simply another scientific advance – if we're happy to use antibiotics why shouldn't we use products from cloning?

Consider the following` quote from the Human Cloning Foundation, which discusses the moral dilemma of holding back research.

> 'The suffering that can be relieved is staggering. This new technology heralds a new era of unparalleled advancement in medicine if people will release their fears and let the benefits begin. Why should another child die from leukaemia when, if the technology is allowed, we should be able to cure it in a few years' time?'
>
> *Human Cloning Foundation*

Arguments to oppose the development of human cloning include:

* human cloning is immoral in that it suggests that some human characteristics are more valuable than others
* cloning could lead to the production of 'designer babies' or a super-race of humans that are designed perfectly
* scientists will continue to push research until they are able to clone entire humans and can't be trusted to limit their work
* therapeutic cloning involves taking human life at an early stage and destroying it for our benefit
* cloning destroys the individual nature of the human race.

What is the future for cloning and genetic research? There are certainly many potential benefits but are the ethical issues and problems too huge to be overcome? Will we end up as a race of clones or replicants, such as you might find in a sci-fi novel, or is the only way we can maintain human nature to avoid cloning?

You need to consider who holds opinions, such as these.

Try to research a wider range of points of view regarding cloning. You could start with biotechnology companies, Genewatch UK, Life and the Human Cloning Foundation.

Science and technology

KEY SKILLS

The arguments surrounding cloning and genetics would make a good focus for a Level 3 IT project. Remember, you need to plan how you will access information sources carefully, for IT3.1.

GURU TIP

It's worth knowing about some of the ways in which governments are controlling research into cloning and how these may be threatened. Start with the British government and see where you can go from there.

KEY SKILLS
IT3

Genetically engineered crops

Genetically engineered food might seem like a bit of mouthful to get your head around. It's something you often hear about and might conjure up images of 'Frankenstein foods'. It could change the world we live in radically - so you need to know what it's all about.

In a General Studies exam you might be asked to sum up the arguments for and against a scientific issue such as GE food, or to answer some questions about a stimulus article. It's the sort of issue that examiners love - there's no right or wrong answer, they're interested in your ability to form a fact-based, balanced argument. It's a topic that's in the news a lot, so you shouldn't have too much trouble finding out a bit about it.

What's a gene?

Genes are made up of DNA. A number of genes together produce different species. It is the different genetic patterns produce by the species that creates the differences between them.

How does GE food work?

People have been modifying plants for hundreds of years by breeding individuals with characterisitics to produce offspring that hopefully have inherited these characterisitics. This is how nectarines were produced – by breeding a hairless peach. New varieties of plants can be created – whether these are a particular colour of rose or a vine which can resist frost better and so is able to be grown in Britain. The products of this sort of breeding can be useful and allow farmers to make greater profits.

> **Getting confused?**
> Genetically Engineered (GE) Food is pretty much the same thing as Genetically Modified (GM) Food.

Genetic engineering of crops has the same aim as selective breeding, in that it aims to produce a better variety of plant. It involves taking genes from one species and inserting them into another. Genes can be taken from plants, bacteria, viruses, insects, animals or even humans in order to engineer new crop varieties. A commonly-quoted example is selecting a gene, which produces a chemical with anti-freeze properties, from an arctic fish and inserting it into a tomato to make it frost-resistant. This extends the growing season for outdoor tomatoes or strawberries so that you can have more of your favourite products throughout the year.

This is fundamentally different from traditional breeding. The British government defines genetic engineering as 'the altering of the genetic material in that organism in a way that does not occur naturally by mating or natural recombination or both'. Genetic engineering is also much quicker and more effective than traditional methods. Selective breeding can take generations to produce the desired effect and is dependent on chance – a different feature might be bred rather than the one farmers are hoping for. Sometimes a feature is inherited that isn't desirable. Breeding has transformed poodles from hunting dogs to miniature dogs that are pretty to look at and can be kept in small homes but the side-effects of this selective breeding include kneecaps that slip out of place and hips that can collapse easily.

GURU TIP
There's a more detailed explanation of genes on page 74.

GURU TIP
Everyone has a vague understanding about GE foods. In order to impress examiners you have to be able to do more than just make a couple of simple arguments based on what you heard on the news one day.

GURU WEBSITE
Test your knowledge on the genetics quiz on the AS Guru™ website at:
www.bbc.co.uk/asguru

Which GE crops are being used at the moment?

Monsanto is a biotechnology compnay that researches the use of genetically engineered crops and related products, such as weed-killer. They developed a variety of soya bean that is resistant to its top selling weed-killer, Round Up. This is an advantage to farmers as they can use Round Up to kill weeds in fields of soya without fear of damaging their crop, which is now resistant to the weed-killer. More weeds killed means more crops grown, meaning more profit for the farmer.

It also means more profit for Monsanto – farmers now have to buy two products from the company. There is great concern about companies, such as Monsanto, gaining a monopoly and dominating the market by making their products so useful for farmers.

> **Remember**
>
> When you read facts like these, try not to defend or criticise the subject (Monsanto) instantly. Think about it logically and remember that the aim of any compnay is to make a profit.

Key facts: GE foods

- GE food has been produced since around 1983.
- In 1998 27 million hectares of land were used to grow GE crops world-wide (excluding China).
- The largest world producers of GE food are USA, Canada and China.
- GE Crops are grown in more than 40 countries – in Britain crop trials are expected to last until at least 2002.
- The most common GE crops include tomatoes, maize and soya beans, all of which are widely used in food processing. As a result GE crops can be present in manufactured foods.
- Biotechnology companies are largely responsible for the development of GE crops.

People simply can't agree about GE food. Biotechnology companies say it's perfectly safe whilst campaigners argue that there hasn't been sufficient testing and that crops could cause major environmental damage. You need to develop your own opinions based upon a full understanding of the arguments used by both sides of the debate. As always, make sure you can provide a balanced answer for an examiner. In the following pages, some of the key arguments are discussed and you should use these to consider the opinions, in developing your own.

> **Research focus:**
>
> Biotechnology companies working in the UK include Monsanto and Aventis. You could research one of these companies to find out how they argue their case and what their other products are. Other places to find different opinions are:
>
> - pressure groups, such as Greenpeace
> - informed media reports – *New Scientist* is a good technical starting point
> - US sources are interesting to look at – they tend to be much more in favour of genetically engineered food. You can access American newspapers on the Internet – try searching through their archives for articles.

GURU TIP
Using short examples like this will impress examiners – it shows that you know what you're talking about. Try to find some others to use.

KEY SKILLS
Searching for information like this, on the web, is a good way to provide evidence for Key Skill IT3.

Science and technology

GURU TIP
It's important to be able to balance your point of view with the opposing one in an exam.

GE foods: forming the argument

GURU TIP

These are just some of the arguments used for and against GE food. Try to research them in a little more depth and add to the list of arguments. Be careful that the sources you use are trustworthy – there can be an awful lot of myths or distorted facts presented by both sides of the argument.

KEY SKILLS
C3

KEY SKILLS

These arguments would make a good complex subject for the Key Skill C3

Biodiversity is the number of different species in an environment. The more species present, the higher the biodiversity. If species become extinct biodiversity declines – and in general high biodiversity is seen as a good thing.

Arguments for and against GE foods

The table below, presents the major arguments used by different groups to support their point of view about GE Food. Think about which groups might use which arguments. Which arguments are environmental and which economic or social? Ultimately, you need to consider which set of arguments are closer to your own opinion and which could you use to argue against your own.

Arguments for GE crop production

- Crops could be developed with resistance to problems, such as drought, disease and pests. This could produce greater crop yields, allowing farmers to produce more food.

- The world needs GE crops to help feed the growing population.

- GE crops mean that less chemicals need to be used, reducing agricultural pollution.

- Crops which are beneficial to human health could be developed – bananas are being engineered to deliver vaccines to diseases, such as Hepatitis B and diarrhoea, making it easier to distribute medicine to children.

- GE food is tested before it's used commercially – non-GE food isn't. This may make GE food safer.

Arguments against GE crop production

- GE crops could lead to genetic changes in other species through cross-pollination – in the US, pollen from GE maize has caused damage to caterpillars of the Monarch butterfly and organic maize has been contaminated by GE maize.

- GE seeds are expensive. The genetic revolution is, therefore, unlikely to solve hunger in poorer, developing countries.

- GE crops may increase the amount of pesticides and herbicides used, increasing agricultural pollution.

- Biodiversity could be reduced if single crops replace existing ecosystems. Scientists in Britain think this could eliminate species such as skylarks if their food is destroyed.

- Are GE crops the thin end of the wedge, leading towards widespread genetic manipulation – perhaps even of human beings?

In an exam you'll often get stimulus material to read and respond to. This could happen in any area of the course so you need to be able to read it quickly and identify the key points. This is a skill you'll probably have used at GCSE – perhaps in English or History.

The article (on the opposite page) is in favour of GE foods. Read it through and identify what the key points are – you could underline these or highlight them as you might in an exam. Then try and write a short paragraph about each of the points saying why you either agree or disagree with it. There are two examples of this within the article, shown in the white boxes. This sort of exercise will help you sharpen your opinion about this issue.

Why I'm happy to Eat GM Food

An opinion poll conducted last year for the International Food Information Council asked the public in Europe and America a deliberately idiotic question: "Would you eat food that contained any genes?" They got a predictably stupid answer - two thirds said no.

It could be that respondents misunderstood and thought they were being asked about denim. More likely, they were replying honestly - and that is the big problem with the great row about GM food. It is impossible to have a rational debate about the issue because of the hysteria raised by the mere mention of the G-word - the meaning of which few of us have the slightest inkling.

On GM crops, science has a powerful case. The charge that genetically modifying organisms tampers with nature is true. We have always done so.

Selective breeding has altered nature – e.g. frost resistant vines. This is not the same thing as Genetic Engineering as the internal composition of the plant is not changed radically. GE is much more immediate and controlled and is not natural.

Nature is not a benign force that is out to protect homo sapiens. Jenner defied nature - and, many thought, common sense - when he began looking at cowpox. Antibiotics defy "natural" bacteria which, left alone, kill us. If the Prince of Wales had been around 100 years ago he would probably have told the Wright brothers that if God had wanted man to fly he would have given us wings. Using new knowledge to do the same task, more precisely and more skilfully, that farmers have done for hundreds of years through the comparative guesswork of cross-breeding does not seem any more "unnatural" than breeding new strains of wheat by traditional means - or indeed new breeds of cattle.

Personally, I would prefer to eat food produced by GM - about 80 per cent of the stuff on US supermarket shelves - than most organic merchandise, none of which has gone through the rigorous testing standards demanded of GM products. Also, I would hope some polling organisation would ask the public, "Do you want to eat food covered in horse dung?" and show the findings to health food shops. There are serious environmental concerns and the jury is still out on them. The sensible response is to hold more trials, not halt them. So far there has been not a single respectable scientific body anywhere in the world that has declared a GM crop now in cultivation to be a danger to the ecosystem.

GE Food is very commonplace in the US where it is much more accepted. Americans often wonder why we get so worked up about the whole issue.

The prime purpose of GM technology in agriculture has so far been to create crops that had in-built resistance to pests. Lowering the use of toxic pesticides was a loud demand by the Green movement until their eyes turned to GM technology. It is only scientists who offer the Third World genuine hopes of relief from hunger. They see agriculture the way it really is - a vast industrialised business in the West, hand-to-mouth scrabbling around on poor land almost everywhere else. Prince Charles' ilk see it as a Hovis ad, the way it has not been for generations here and never in Africa.

The worst mistake, though, would be to give in to the call to halt GM testing, rigorously and independently controlled. Without open research and inquiry we do not have science. And without science we don't have civilisation.

Science and technology

GURU TIP

If you're looking for articles about other issues to use in General Studies try newspapers or news websites. The BBC site is a good place to start – you can search for old stories if there's an issue you're particularly interested in.

GURU TIP

For more on Jenner take a look at the What is science? section on page 54.

The benefits to less economically developed countries (LEDCs) are often used to support GE Food. Is this a valid argument? Are GE Foods being used in LEDCs? It's worth looking into what the charities, who work with these countries, have to say.

GM food: what does the future hold?

GURU TIP

Continue to think about your point of view when you read the arguments. What could you use to support it and what could be used to attack it in an exam?

In the article on the previous page, Victor Sebestyen puts forward his arguments to back up his opinion that GE Food is probably safe to eat and that we should continue crop trials to make sure that it is. How do people who disagree with him put forward their opinions?

The following article is from the Prince of Wales' website and explains some of the reasons why he is opposed to GE Foods.

What sort of world do we want to live in?

This is the biggest question of all. I raise it because the capacity of GM technology to change our world has brought us to a crossroads of fundamental importance. Are we going to allow the industrialisation of life itself, redesigning the natural world for the sake of convenience and embarking on an Orwellian future?

Or should we be adopting a gentler, more considered approach, seeking always to work with the grain of Nature in making better, more sustainable use of what we have, for the long-term benefit of mankind as a whole? The answer is important. It will affect far more than the food we eat; it will determine the sort of world that we, and our children, inhabit.

Orwellian relates to George Orwell's view of future societies in his novel, *1984,* where virtually all aspects of life were controlled by the State. It suggests a 'Big Brother' type of approach – always being watched – and where governments and companies can control every aspect of the world.

A good follow up activity to use here would be to outline two or more arguments that might be developed to support Prince Charles' point of view on GE food. Use the information you have to work on the opinions that counter Victor Sebestyen's view that GE Food is worth developing.

Most arguments used by GE protestors focus on the potential environmental impacts. The TV programme which accompanies this book goes so far as to suggest that 'It's hard to disagree with the commercial and moral arguments in favour of GM crops, when it could make the difference between life and death in the developing world'. Victor Sebestyen uses the same argument. Is this really the case?

At this point, it is important to consider the more alternative views. Some important opinions to remember are:

- seeds may be too expensive for the farmers in LEDCs to purchase
- biotechnology companies need to make money, cover their research costs and are answerable to their share holders
- small farmers may be put out of business and large corporations will take over agriculture, due to increasing costs associated with GE crops
- GE crops could mean that people won't be in control of their own lives and what they consume, this is an important aspect of sustainable development.

Organic vs GE food
Organic products are grown without any artificial substances (such as fertiliser or herbicides) added. They are essentially 'natural' products. Genetic Engineering isn't natural. Organic products are totally different to GE ones.

How far should protestors go to stop GE Food?

This article, from the BBC News website (http://news.bbc.co.uk/hi/english/uk/), deals with the trial of protestors accused of destroying Norfolk GE trial crops. You could summarise what their arguments are likely to be.

Jury discharged in GM crop case

The jury in the trial of 28 Greenpeace protesters accused of damaging genetically modified crops has been discharged after failing to reach a verdict.

Verdict
The protestors were later found innocent, in a retrial, on the basis of 'lawful excuse'.

They argued that they had a lawful excuse to destroy the crop because they believed that organic crops cultivated nearby were in need of protection. On arrest several defendants had told police they had acted to prevent the 'genetic pollution' of other crops by the GM maize.

One of the 28 accused, Baptist minister Malcolm Carroll, told the hearing he took part in the action out of a sense of Christian duty. Christians in general agree that there is a higher order that you can never violate. But there are occasions where there are actions that are unjust or dangerous for some reason and there is a set of circumstances which may call for peaceful direct action

What evidence could protestors use to back up their claims about genetic pollution? How seriously do you think these claims should be taken?

> **Confusing chemicals?**
> Herbicides kill plants - usually weeds. Pesticides kill pests that might eat crops - insects, for example. Both chemicals are used to increase crop yields.

Finding the answer

The subject of genetically modified crops is a long way from being resolved. Both sides of the argument are strongly defensible. The best way to develop opinions is to find out as much as possible about every issue surrounding the topic, quite a mammoth task when you consider the economic, social, political, religious and development angles. It's important to keep in mind the reasons why an organisation might be releasing reports in the subject. You should try and think about their motivation in order to uncover any bias in the reporting. Are there any facts that have been missed out or presented in a particular way, in order to support a particular point of view? Statistics can be misleading if you don't read them carefully.

GE food is an issue, which is certain to remain in the newspapers for the foreseeable future. It's current, controversial and confusing. It's also topical enough to be the sort of topic that examiners will ask questions on! It's a great chance to prove that you have a balanced knowledge of the facts and opinions and can argue your case concisely.

How far do you agree with Malcolm Carroll's opinion that some circumstances call for peaceful direct action? This would make a great General Studies question!

GURU TIP
How can statistics mislead? Think about an advert that tells you that 4 out of 5 people preferred a particular product. Think about how many people were asked and how many expressed a view. Was there a cross-section of people?

Science and technology

Practice questions

You could face a variety of questions in the science and technology section of your exam. It will often include short answer or multiple choice questions. In multiple choice questions, make sure you pick just one of the answers Develop your confidence by working through past or sample papers.

GURU TIP

Use brief examples – if 3 or 4 marks are available, you need to make 3 or 4 solid points, but keep it short. If 6–10 marks are available, you need to write a couple of paragraphs and make several relevant points.

With very short questions, state the facts quickly and efficiently. Don't write lots for 1 mark, but be accurate.

Most specifications have a question about graphs. This may not be part of the science and technology questions.

You can also expect to get questions on passages of text – perhaps about scientific discoveries or issues.

1 Which answer is a correct statement about genetically engineered crops?
   (a) They are produced by adding genes from one species to another.
   (b) They are produced by breeding different species together.
   (c) They are produced naturally.
   (d) They can only be produced in test tubes.

2 State what role the ozone layer plays in the earth's atmosphere (1 mark).

3 Name the scientist who developed the theory of evolution (1 mark).

4 Outline two points used to justify genetically engineered crops (4 marks).

5 Outline two arguments used to support the opinion that nuclear power is a danger to the biosphere (4 marks).

6 Briefly describe how scientific method advances scientific knowledge (6 marks).

7 What are the main limitations of scientific inductive methods (6 marks)?
   They may revolve around text or figures or require longer, essay-style answers.

8 Study the graph. It shows the global temperature changes in the 20th Century.

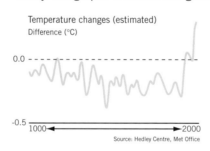

Temperature changes (estimated) Difference (°C)

Source: Hedley Centre, Met Office

   (a) How much was the temperature above normal in 1988 (1 mark)?
   (b) How has global temperature changed during the 20th century (4 marks)?
   (c) How do scientists think global warming is being caused (4 marks)?
   (d) Why it is difficult to prove that global warming is happening (6–10 marks)?

9 How would you find out if your food is genetically modified (6-10 marks)?

10 What methods could be used to communicate with a friend living in mainland Europe (6-10 marks)?

Depending upon your exam board, longer questions could be worth 10–40 marks. You need to write an essay-style answer with an introduction, several paragraphs developing your argument and a conclusion that answers the question

11 'Evolution is only a theory.' Critically examine the arguments which may be made in support of this claim.

12 'Science is not at fault. If the inventions of scientists are misused it is societies fault not that of science.' How far do you agree with this statement?

13 Evaluate the arguments for and against burning fossil fuels

14 Should scientists be allowed to use any means, in order to benefit humanity?

15 'Technology always advances society.' For an example you have studied, provide evidence which either supports or undermines this claim.

Society, politics and the economy

In this section you will learn about:

☞ the origins and role of value systems in contemporary life in the UK

☞ relationships between ethical and value systems and the law

☞ the main institutions of political life in the UK

☞ the role and character of the main political parties in the UK

☞ the development of the Welfare State in the UK

☞ how the National Health Service has evolved

☞ global economic inequality

☞ international debt and aid and their relationship with poverty.

This section discusses economics, international affairs, the law, politics and sociological argument. It looks at complex questions that are dealt with, by society and by individuals, such as health, education and poverty. These are all affected by society, politics and the economy. You may be surprised by how many sources of information you can draw on to help you in this section of the course:

• other AS level subjects, such as history, geography, sociology, politics or economics
• television and radio news and the Internet
• your own experiences with the National Health Service
• some aspects of the issues may have been raised in personal and social development classes.

Prior knowledge, experience and opinions are valuable in AS General Studies. It's important to take a position and state your views, but the key to success is to place those opinions under scrutiny. Think about the logic and strength of your own argument. Don't be afraid to find fault with it, or to accept evidence that challenges your assumptions and conclusions. By strengthening both sides of the argument in your mind and on the page, you can successfully tackle the weaknesses and limitations.

As you read through this section:

• think about how you are affected by the issues
• listen, next time you hear one of the issues on the radio or television
• make sure you understand both sides of the argument
• pick a few subjects that really interest you and research them further.

Values in society

Many of the questions you will face in AS General Studies directly or indirectly link to the issue of values in UK society. Broadly, 'values' refers to issues that are not just about individuals' preferences, but collective ideas about what constitutes a 'good' society and a 'good' life. Good is not the same as 'nice' or 'pleasant' in this context, it is about rights and wrongs.

Frameworks of values and **moral** thinking are important in General Studies in a number of ways. Most importantly, they shape people's perceptions (how they view the world) and their actions (what they actually do). In many General Studies questions you will need to be able to identify the different values of different commentators and groups in a social debate; you will also want to be able to understand how those values influence their actions.

What are values?

What do you think might motivate the following actions?

> A Quaker who refuses to fight in a war?

> A person giving money to a voluntary organisation, such as Oxfam?

A Quaker is a member of the Society of Friends – a Christian movement that embraces simple living and pacificsm.

You might think that the Quaker is a coward and just looking to save his skin, or that the Oxfam donor is making himself feel less guilty about his wealth. They could both be looking after self-centred interests.

Equally, you might argue that both the Quaker and the donor are being guided by their values, or moral beliefs: that it is fundamentally wrong to take part in acts of violence against anyone; or that is right for the rich and the privileged to pass on some of their wealth to those who have less.

Both answers could be right simultaneously, since most human behaviour is driven by a combination of individual interests and values or moral beliefs. It is much more important to be able to point out these different standpoints and opinions in a debate, than to be able to offer a definitive answer.

What's the difference between values and morals?

Values are what you find important in society. Morals are the way you behave because of your values. In fact, it's hard to separate the two. For example, if you believe in freedom as the most important social good, you'll value democratic government, and might well support economic freedoms as well.

Where do values come from?

Where values and moral beliefs come from and how they develop is a complex thing. On one hand, they are created, chosen and adapted by individuals. On the other, everyone draws upon a whole range of value systems for making moral sense of the world. To understand the contemporary moral landscape of the UK, it's worth taking a brief look at history.

Up to the 17th Century	For most of the last millennium, the single, dominant moral framework in the UK was Christianity. Until the 17th Century, at the earliest, no moral debate could take place without referring to the core beliefs and teachings of the Christian churches.
Beyond the 17th Century	In the following centuries, Christianity as a moral framework began to be less solid, as the Church fragmented between Protestants and Catholics. Christianity was also challenged by secular (non-religious) political ideologies: these tried to explain the world; describe what a better, moral world would be like; and find ways to bring that world about in this life (not in an afterlife, as religions often did).
18th, 19th and early 20th Century	The main political ideologies of these Centuries were conservatism, liberalism and socialism (see definitions of these ideologies below). All continued in some ways to draw upon Christianity, and they still provide the main frameworks for thinking about moral, economic and political issues in the 21st Century

Political ideologies

These notes describe the general tendencies of different political views. They do not relate specifically to UK political parties although, of course, there are significant connections between, for example, **conservative** ideas and the culture and policy of the Conservative party.

It is important to note that the three political **ideologies**, listed below, do not cover all the different ideas about politics. Other forms of political thinking include anarchism, environmentalism and feminism. All of these political movements overlap and interact with each other but the following three ideologies have formed the core of mainstream political argument in this country for over 100 years.

Once you have read through and understood this section on values in society, try and work through the ideas again, using the section on political parties, on page 94, to get a better insight into the motives and driving forces in our political system.

Conservatism
- values the past, stability and order as the primary 'goods' of a society.
- believes these are best achieved by valuing a dislike of change, the importance of power, hierarchies of power, and wisdom.

Liberalism
- prioritises the individual over the collective; and freedoms and rights over any other political or social good.
- advocates a sharp distinction between public and private moral values.
- argues that the areas in which collective moral regulation is more important than individuals' preferences should be as limited as possible.

Socialism
- argues that freedoms and rights are not enough to guarantee a good society.
- values are based on ideas of equality and solidarity treating everybody the same
- individual freedoms must be restricted where they would undermine these features of society.

GURU TIP
When you come across policy ideas or arguments from the political parties, try and ask yourself what political and moral value systems they might be drawing on.

Values today

In the late 20th Century, certain shifts occurred to change the moral landscape:

- Britain has shifted from being mainly a Christian society to being a multi-faith one, with significant numbers of Hindus, Jews and Muslims
- mainstream Christian churches have seen the number of members decline greatly, along with their influence in the public sphere, a process called secularisation
- the mainstream political ideologies all faced problems in presenting a coherent set of moral arguments that attracted large numbers of supporters
- fewer people joined political parties, or declared allegiance to a party
- these traditional systems of thought don't seem to be able to provide satisfactory moral answers to contemporary problems
- there are more alternative (or 'fringe') moral frameworks with groups of supporters
- recent decades have seen the expansion of fundamentalist and evangelical Christianity in the UK; a range of alternative religious and spiritual practices, from druids, to scientologists; and the development of new political ideologies, such as feminism and environmentalism.

Values – a source of support or conflict?

Moral and value systems can have positive effects within a society.

- provide an identity for individuals who accept particular moral teachings and values, and help them to feel part of a wider social group. It forms a social bond which leads to empathy and support for the people involved. People like to describe themselves as Muslims or liberals or environmentalists.
- create the basis for action, both individual actions (e.g. deciding to become vegetarian); and collective action (e.g. protesting with others about the export of live cattle for slaughter).
- However, In a society with a lot of different value systems, religious and secular, there will be certain conflicts, partly caused by the effects mentioned above:
- it's harder to achieve a universal consensus on moral arguments because there are so many different opinions.
- it's difficult for adherents of any value system to claim moral superiority over others.

This does not mean that there are no moral agreements; or that all values and morals can automatically be considered equally valuable or right; or that agreement on a collective moral life has become impossible – though some relativists might argue this.

Rather, it is that moral life has become more complicated and there's more need of finding ways in which differences can be aired, understood and negotiated.

Consider the debate about the morning after pill.

The morning after pill is a form of contraception. Women can prevent a pregnancy, by taking the drug within a few days of intercourse. The labour government has decided to make the this pill more easily available. It is now available, over the counter, in chemists, rather than having to get a prescription from a GP. In particular, it will be available to 16 year olds, without any contact with a GP or families being necessary. As you might expect, very different attitudes coming from very different value systems exist on this issue. Some of the main points are listed on the following page.

- Some people are worried that this 'safety net' will increase unprotected sexual activity among young people.
- Some people believe that parents and guardians have the right to know what drugs under-18s are taking.
- other people believe that this is the best way to reduce the large number of unwanted teenage pregnancies and that young people have the right to privacy and control over reproduction.

> **Research focus:** keep a look out for stories in the press on moral dilemmas and debates. See if you can use the material here to identify which moral frameworks and values are being used in the dispute.

Can these differences of opinion be resolved? Watch out for this story in the news, it's a highly controversial topic that people have very strong opinions about. It is also a subject that you should form an opinion on. The best way to do this, is to listen to everybody's points of view and make up your own mind, based on the facts.

New moral issues

Modern Britain is changing and is almost incomparable with the Britain of a few decades ago. The diversity in all areas of our society, from religion, to tradition, to food and culture, has produced a complex blend of values and morals.

The British value systems are having to cope with new moral and practical issues. The pace of technological and social change keeps throwing up new dilemmas. For example:

- should research be allowed on human embryos?
- should parents be able to screen their unborn children genetically for physical and mental disabilities?
- should human societies include the world's ecosystem in their moral thinking? How? As family structures change and multiply, can you still argue that one kind of family is best or morally superior?

GURU TIP
Do you have a filing system for cuttings from the press? Try and create one, so that you can refer to specific examples while you are working through the course.

Society, politics and the economy

What is relativism?
In its extreme form, relativism describes the idea that all moral positions are of equivalent value and worth. Also, no procedures exist for choosing between them.

The UK political system

What is politics?

One way to think about it is to consider all the activities and institutions involved in regulating social life - the formal and informal making and monitoring of rules that govern what everybody does and how they interact. If you look at it like this, politics in its widest sense is not just about politicians and governments.

> **Research focus:** think about the politics of your own family. Ask, who has the power to make what rules, can people resist, or refuse to obey the rules? What sanctions, punishments, bribes and deals are possible when it comes to deciding who will tidy up or who will do the washing up?

This section, however, looks at politics in a narrower sense: the politics that revolve around the State of the United Kingdom. Note that states are not the same thing as governments. States are the collection of institutions and offices that make, enforce and monitor the binding laws and rules of a society. They ultimately maintain their authority by being the only organisation that can legitimately or rightfully use force, such as the police force and armies.

Governments are just the groups of people at the very top of this great cluster of organisations who temporarily try to run the machine.

What is a constitution?

The basis of most political systems is a constitution.

A constitution is the basic rules and regulations that govern political life. In modern societies, such as the UK, this mainly refers to the rules that govern the State. Constitutions set out:

- which State institutions have which powers
- who makes the rules
- who enforces the rules
- how those institutions are to be established and run
- which posts will be elected and which will be non-elected and how non-elected posts will be appointed.

Constitutions also set out the nature of the relationship between a state and its citizens. Some constitutions include the Bill of Individual Rights and limited state intrusions into people's lives.

Written and unwritten constitutions

You may have heard people say that the UK is unusual in that it has an 'unwritten constitution'. Well, what does this mean?

Different societies have different ways of setting out their constitution. Most, nowadays, possess a written constitution. This usually means that it is set down in a single, defining document. The UK has what is called an unwritten constitution, but this doesn't mean that it hasn't been put down on paper, so you can't look up the rules and regulations of political life. It just reflects the fact that it draws on many different sources of authority, often, but not always, written down, and usually produced at different times in history, dealing with different aspects of political life.

GURU TIP

Have you ever heard on the news that a judges decision is awaited with great interest, because it will set a precendent? That's because once a judgement has been made, future cases can point to that judgement in support of their case – if they are hoping for the same outcome.

Sources of the UK Constitution

The unwritten UK Constitution is drawn from a variety of sources, below are some examples.

- Legislation (law): the composition of the electorate is laid down in various Representation of the People Acts.
- Common Law: accumulated custom based on previous legal decisions, for example the principal of judicial review, in which the courts can question whether State business has been carried out by the correct procedure.
- European Union Law: since 1973, when the UK signed the Treaty of Rome and joined the European Union, European law has increasingly become the basis of much constitutional law in the UK.
- Convention: these are the genuinely unwritten rules that politics relies upon in the UK to function smoothly. For example, by law, the Monarch can call anyone to form a government after a general election, but by convention it is always the leader of the biggest party in the House of Commons that is invited to do so.
- Law and Custom of Parliament: the Houses of Parliament draw up and implement their own internal rules of operation.

Key features of the UK Constitution

The UK Constitution can be characterised as:

- Unitary rather than Federal. This means that legally-defined power ultimately lies in a single place (the Houses of Parliament) and is not divided up between several institutions (the Church or the army, for instance).
- Parliamentary Sovereignty over Popular Sovereignty. This means that power ultimately lies with Parliament and its representatives elected by the people, and not with the Prime Minster and Cabinet or with all the people as individuals.

The institutions that make up the UK State

Another way of looking at the constitution, is to divide up what different institutions do. The Government consists of three different groups: the Legislature, the Executive and the Judiciary. Here is what each of these does:

- **The Legislature** in the UK is the Houses of Parliament. It is made up of the elected members of the House of Commons and the appointed members of the House of Lords. The Commons is elected by universal suffrage: this means that everyone over the age of 18 can vote. General elections must happen at least every five years, but the Prime Minister can call one whenever he or she likes within that time. The Legislature spends most of its time writing, examining and passing the laws of the land. Its other key task is to keep an eye on the Executive.
- **The Executive** consists of the people and institutions who actually run the State and carry out the orders of the lawmakers. In the UK, the Executive is a hybrid made up of politicians and the Civil Service. When their Party wins a General Election for the House of Commons, the politicians are formally asked by the Monarch to form a government.The government consists of the Prime Minister, the Secretaries of State and the junior ministers.
- Finally, keeping an eye on both of the others, is the **Judiciary**. This consists of the judges who, within the existing laws, have the final say about what rules mean (especially when they are ambiguous), and rule on who has or has not broken them. Judges are appointed, rather than elected, though the Executive has ultimate control over their appointment - this is a responsibility of the Lord Chancellor, who is a member of the Cabinet and the House of Lords.

GURU TIP

The Houses of Parliament are often referred to as 'Westminster'.

'Whitehall' refers to the government ministries and the Civil Service.

The members of our political system, that you hear about most often, are all part of the Executive. Each member has a specific political part to play.

The Executive is headed by the Prime Minister, who is conventionally, but not automatically, the leader of the biggest party in the House of Commons. The Secretaries of State run different Ministries (the Home Office, for example) and form the Cabinet. The Cabinet holds the Prime Minister's key advisers and is the central committee of the government. The rest of the Executive is made up of the junior ministers, whose role will depend on which department of state.

But all of these are just a new 'board of directors' in a bigger organisation. Civil Servants hold permanent jobs in the Ministries and work to advise whichever government is in power and help it to carry out its policies.

The context of politics

The central state institutions described above are not the whole of political life or the political system. They are constrained in what they can do by other institutions, both political and non-political.

Firstly, states have to live in the world and the world is made up of other states; international organisations, such as the World Bank; global financial and trading markets; flows of refugees; and global issues, such as the atmosphere and oceans.

Closer to home, the UK is part of the European Union. Being a member creates opportunities to influence European institutions and politics, but also shapes UK laws and practices

If these constraints are 'above' the UK State, then there are also political influences and constraints 'below' it. The UK State has recently devolved power to elected political institutions in Scotland (a Parliament) Wales (an Assembly) and Northern Ireland (an Assembly). There are also several tiers of local government all over the UK.

The government must also talk to and negotiate with interest groups that represent sections of the population united by shared political and social interests – such as business organisations, or workers in trade unions. It must also engage with pressure groups, formed by sections of the population with shared values – such as environmental or religious groups.

In addition, every four or five years, the politicians have to go back to the general public to be re-elected in a General Election.

KEY SKILLS

Working on the UK political system gives you the opportunity to work on Key Skill C3.3. After you have read through this section, write two documents based on the material covered. The first should be an extended piece of writing that addresses the question:

To what extent is the UK constitution a source of poltical division and political problems?

You should then write a short set of revision notes – no more that 150 words on the same topic.

Research focus: can the old institutions cope with some of the new complexities and demands of modern life?

Is Parliament, for example, the right place to decide what is safe and what is dangerous with regard to environmental risks? Are the political parties still able to represent us adequately on these issues?

Once you've read through this section on politics, use the Internet and reference books to form your own opinion on the future of our current political system. Do you think that it's time for change? If a single, defining, written constitution were to be drawn up, what would you like to see included?

Current debates

Much day-to-day politics in the UK is about very practical and immediate issues, such as:

- how much tax will people pay?
- how much money should be spent on the Health Service?
- what should be the content of the National Curriculum?

But, increasingly, UK political life is also about some of the bigger questions raised by the structure and operation of the political system as a whole.

The break-up of Britain

For some, the devolution of power from the centre to the nations is only the first step in the political break-up of the UK. Many Nationalists in Scotland and Wales would like to separate entirely from the UK. Consider these questions:

- Even if Scotland and Wales do remain part of the UK, can the old institutions cope with the new order?
- Should Scottish and Welsh MPs continue to vote on English legislation in the House of Commons, when English MPs no longer vote on Scottish and Welsh issues, for example?

The quality of democracy

- Is one vote at a general election every four or five years, for a limited range of political parties, enough **democracy**?
- Does the UK need a new electoral system that would give parties a share of power that is closer to their share of the vote?
- Should there be new ways for the Legislature and Judiciary to regulate and monitor the very powerful Executive?

Global versus local

- If a great deal of power is wielded over politics by institutions and processes that are global, or European, do people in the UK have democratic control over them?
- Who votes for the financial markets? Who actually knows what the World Bank is up to?

Local government

- Local government in the UK is quite weak; is strongly regulated by the centre and doesn't have much control over its finances.
- Should there be more powerful local government, with more power to raise its own money?

Try thinking about and discussing some of these issues. Arm yourself with facts and opinions on both sides of the arguments. Be prepared to present a debate on Political issues and express a well thought-out point of view.

GURU TIP

Many of these issues will be discussed in the newspapers. Try and skim through the papers once a week and cut out one story or article that relates to these big political debates.

GURU TIP

There is another section in this book that looks at the current strengths and weaknesses of political parties. See pages 96–97.

GURU TIP

It's worth your time finding out about contemporary politics in the lead up to your exams. Try reading at least one article a day on UK politics, from a broadsheet newspaper. Find out who your local MP is and who your local councillors are. If there's an issue that you feel strongly about, research it and try writing a letter to them or even try and arrange a meeting.

Society, politics and the economy

UK political parties

Like them or not, political parties are almost unavoidable in AS General Studies. You will get asked about many aspects of social and political life and political parties are invariably involved in the debates around them and any government action or inaction on the issue.

What is a political party?

The main thing that attracts people to a political party is power. Political parties are permanent organisations which represent a set of ideas and interests that their members have in common. The parties seek to win, hold and execute political power so that they can further these ideas and interests.

In the UK, political parties win power by standing at and winning elections for governing institutions. These institutions include:

- local government
- Scottish Parliament
- Welsh Assembly
- Northern Irish Assembly
- House of Commons
- European Parliament.

The functions of political parties

Political parties in the UK perform a number of jobs. How well they do them is worth thinking about and debating. Here are some of their functions:

Political representation

Political parties represent you in the governing institution. You give your vote in return for their commitment to broadly argue a case and pursue policies that you approve of.

Communication

Political parties spend a lot more time and trouble thinking about politics than most of us. They can, therefore, act as communicators, keeping the general public informed of the options and problems that collectively face us.

Interest aggregation

If every different political position was represented separately in politics, the cacophony of disagreement would probably make decision-making impossible. Political parties exist to gather together people with recognisably similar political positions into more manageable groups. Of course, they want to attract as many people as possible to their group to make it as strong and influential as possible, so one of their jobs is to persuade people to join them.

Political recruitment

Political parties also provide a channel or career path for those people who actually want to become politicians. Running as an independent is fearsomely difficult and complicated. Political parties are organisations that can support and help promote potential politicians.

Political participation

Not everyone who is interested in politics and joins a political party wants to be a politician or run for office; but parties provide an opportunity for those who don't want a career out of politics to participate in the process as active citizens.

KEY SKILLS

Working on the websites of political parties (below) gives you an opportunity to show Key Skills IT3.1 and IT3.2.

Use your search through the websites, to do two things:

- find out how many members each political party has

- compare attitudes and policies of the parties on Europe or healthcare, for example.

KEY SKILLS
IT3.1 and IT3.2

GURU TIP

Visit the party websites:

www.conseratives.com
www.uup.org
www.labour.org.uk/
www.libdems.org.uk
www.natdems.org.uk
www.plaidcymru,orgw
www.SDLP.ie
www.sinnfein.org

The party system in the UK

It is helpful not to think about individual political parties in the UK in isolation but to think about the way they interact with and influence each other. This is what is called a party system.

But why have parties at all? Why not just have a lot of individuals and independents standing for office? Why the need for these organisations? There is more to political parties than meets the eye.

Take a look at the electoral data in the figure below and have a go at answering the following questions. The notes on interpreting data below the chart will help. Answers and some commentary are provided on the next page. Try and figure it out before looking!

1. How many parties have actually formed a government?

2. Which party has formed governments most often?

3. Which party has the biggest differences between share of the vote and its share of seats in the House of Commons?

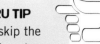

GURU TIP
Don't skip the information shown here, or anywhere, although it may be daunting or off-putting. Take it a bit at a time. You will almost certainly have to eal with some of it in the exam,

| | No. of seats | | % share of vote | |
	Lab.	Con.	Lab.	Con.
1945	393	213	47.8	39.8
1950	315	298	46.1	43.5
1951	297	321	48.8	48.0
1955	277	344	46.4	49.7
1959	258	365	43.8	49.4
1964	317	304	44.1	43.4
1966	363	253	47.9	41.9
1970	287	330	43.0	46.4
1974 (Feb.)	301	297	37.1	37.9
1974 (Oct.)	319	277	39.2	35.8
1979	268	339	36.9	43.9
1983	209	397	27.6	42.4
1987	229	375	30.8	42.3
1992	271	336	34.4	41.9
1997	419	165	43.2	30.7

Votes and seats of the major parties in general elections since 1945.

Interpreting data

You may be asked to interpret data in graph or table form in your AS General Studies. Look carefully at the labels on the table to see exactly what is being shown – are there units (such as percentages or 'hundreds' or 'thousands')? Does it represent a time period – days, months or specific years? Then read the questions you have been asked very carefully. It's easy to give an answer that may be shown in the table or graph, but is not the answer to the question you have been asked.

GURU TIP

See the notes on the opposite page for an overview of the values of the main UK political parties.

KEY SKILLS
N3.2 and N3.3

KEY SKILLS

Think of a way to present this data in a graph to explain the development of the UK political system, to achieve Key Skills N3.2 and N3.3..

The country is divided into hundreds of smaller areas called constituencies.

GURU TIP

In AS General Studies it is important to make sure you know both sides of an argument – in this case both the strengths and the weaknesses of political parties.

Answers and comments

This page looks at possible solutions to the problems, discussed on page 95.

1 Only two parties – Labour and the Conservatives – have actually formed a post-war government. Often, the UK has been described as a 'two-party system', because these two parties are the only ones that ever seem to exercise real power.

2 The Conservatives have formed the most governments and have been in power for the most time since the 2nd World War. Between 1979 and 1997 they were in uninterrupted power with some very large majorities (so that they had many more representatives in Parliament than any other party and could push through legislation without fear of another party, or parties defeating it). Some felt that no other party was capable of winning an election any more and thus the UK might have become a 'dominant party system'.

3 A trend over recent years has been the solid vote for the Liberals or Liberal Democrats, though they have achieved fewer seats than their share of the vote would suggest. This is due to the 'first past the post' system (see below), whereby the politician who wins the most votes in each Constituency is elected. A party's candidates could come a close second in every Constituency and still have no representatives in Parliament. Combined with the Liberal Democrat's strength in local government, this suggests that the UK is becoming a 'two-and-a-half or three party system'.

The Scottish Parliament and Welsh Assemblies have Proportional Representation and significant Nationalist parties. These systems are 'multi-party' – with no single party likely to be able to command a sustainable majority government.

Voting systems

First past the post	In the 'first past the post' system, every voter casts one vote for the candidate (and party) they choose. The votes are counted and the candidate with the most votes wins, in each constituency. Advantages of this system are that it is very straightforward and gives a clear result. Disadvantages are that candidates (and parties) can get many votes but not win any seats – although a lot of people agree with their policies, there is no-one to represent them in Parliament.
Proportional Representation (PR)	There are lots of different PR systems, which try to represent the wishes of the majority of people more fairly, by making the number of votes cast for each party count in the result, rather than picking a winner within each constituency. This usually involves taking account of voters' second choices.

Strengths and weaknesses of political parties

Political parties often tend towards division and conflict rather than unity and cohesion. This ensures debate and the airing of different views within them.

However, political parties often seem remote, arrogant and out of touch with the general public. In particular, many people feel that they would rather offer their support and allegiance to single issue campaigning groups, such as Greenpeace, for example, rather than be involved in the muddy complexities of party politics. Could Greenpeace run the whole country, even if it wanted to? What would happen to economic policy, or education?

Political parties – united they stand, divided they fall

Speaking about political parties as clear and separate groups, as on these pages, suggests that they are completely unified organisations, internally. However, a quick glance at the news suggests that this can be far from true.

In fact, all political parties are loose alliances, made up of different political strands, groups and interests, that are related but by no means everyone in the party holds exactly the same views on every issue. A basic problem for any party that aspires to power is to weld people with different viewpoints into a strong coalition. Internal unity is the first step towards government.

The Labour Party
The Labour Party has, since its creation, been an alliance between its industrial wing of organised labour in the trade union movements and its parliamentary wing.

- In the 1970s the unions were very powerful and had a lot of influence over what the Party stood and fought for. Unions contributed a great deal of money to Labour and so had a strong voice inside the Party.
- In recent years, the power of the trade unions within the party and the importance of their financial contributions has declined. There are still significant ideological differences within the party. Traditional socialists (Old Labour), social democrats (New Labour) and Christian socialists are all part of the Party.

The Conservative Party
The Conservative Party of today is broadly divided between three ideological currents.

- On the left of the party are the 'one-nation' Tories who tend to be pro-Europe and in favour of more generous social policies.
- On the right of the party are the eurosceptics and nationalists who are increasingly opposed to the UK's relationship with the European Union.
- Overlapping with both these wings are the neo-liberals, whose politics are shaped by their commitment to and belief in very orthodox free markets and a small, non-interventionist State.

The Liberal Democrats.
Again, a shared commitment to the principles of liberalism in the Party masks significant differences within.

- The Liberal Democrats have both rural and urban wings;
- they have support from the Celtic nations (Scotland, Wales and Ireland), but their main power-base is in the South of England and London;
- there are economic liberals and strong environmentalists, too.

The Nationalists.
Even the Nationalist parties of Scotland and Wales, united by their commitment to independence, have significant divisions.

- Both the SNP (Scottish Nationalist Party) and PC (Plaid Cymru) are divided by strategy (independence now or later?)
- and there are more conventional left-right differences over economics and social policy.

GURU TIP

Keep a look out for stories in the press about internal party conflicts. See if you can use the material here to identify which faction or part of each party is involved in the dispute.

The 'one nation' Tories are called this because they represent a brand of conservatism that is inclusive rather than exclusive. It puts collective national identity above class differences.

GURU TIP

A non-interventionist state is a model of government, in which state activity is reduced to a minimum level.

Society, politics and the economy

The UK Welfare State

KEY WORDS

Here is a list of terms you are introduced to in this section. Learn when to use them

Welfare State

Public Sector

Private Sector

Liberal, Conservative, Social Democratic Welfare States

The Poor Law

The Beveridge Report

The post-war Consensus

What words and ideas do you associate with The Welfare State?

Jot down the first ideas that come into your head. There are no right answers, but you might have included:

education

health

child benefit

pensions

social security

unemployment benefit

In the UK today, all of these services are mainly provided by the State, or the public sector as it is sometimes called, and paid for out of the money the State receives from taxation. These services are collectively called the Welfare State. Some of these services can also be purchased from charities, companies, private hospitals, private schools, and so on. These organisations are part of what is called the private sector.

Although often in AS General Studies, you will be looking at issues and debates on individual components of the Welfare State, it is important to have an overall view of how the system works. This is important for practical reasons, after all, how can policies on healthcare be separated from policies to provide safe housing, healthy food in schools or benefits that ensure families have enough to eat?

The economic importance of the Welfare State is immense and needs to be thought about in an inter-connected way: The NHS is the country's biggest employer. Social Security adds up to about one third of all UK government expenditure.

Different types of Welfare State

Not all societies provide welfare services and, even when they do, the reasons for providing them and the ways they are provided vary greatly. In most societies, for most of human history, the State has not been involved in providing these services at all. Churches, families, communities and markets are all private companies and have been much more important. However, once societies experience large-scale industrial revolutions certain things tend to happen:

- Governments and companies realise that they need more people to be healthy and educated so that they can serve as soldiers in mass armies and work efficiently in increasingly complex economies.
- Old systems of family and community support break down as rural communities are scattered and huge urban communities emerge.
- People become organised and demand better provision from the government.

These demands and pressures have forced governments to invent and run welfare states. But welfare states comes in a variety of forms, as shown in the table below.

Before the Second World War, the Welfare State in the UK was a mixture of Liberal and Conservative. After the War, it became a mixture of Liberal and Social Democratic welfare. In recent years, it has become less Social Democratic, in some ways.

GURU TIP

Never assume that the way things are done in the UK is the only way of doing things.

Always try and compare the UK model of, for example, welfare states, to other societies.

Liberal welfare states example: USA	These are minimalist welfare states. They seek to provide the minimum of State-run and -funded services for the very poorest groups in society. As far as possible, private insurance and private provision is preferred.
Conservative welfare states example: late 19th Century Germany, Italy	These welfare states, often established by ruling aristocracies and the church, are more generous in their provision and more widespread in their coverage. They are usually designed to supply services in an unequal way, with special attention going to those who support the regime – Civil Servants, for example.
Social Democratic welfare states example: Scandinavian countries	The most generous and universal of welfare states, seeking to provide high-standard services for everyone, funded by high levels of taxation.

Welfare in the UK before 1945

Before the Second World War, the one area where the State was involved in the provision of welfare was the Poor Law. It was established under the Tudors and concerned the collecting of money locally to support the destitute (the elderly without family support, orphans, and so on), often in return for tiring, repetitive work. The Workhouse, as it was known, was deliberately unappealing to discourage people from wanting to go there and to keep the cost to the local ratepayers down.

By the late 19th Century, the vast populations of the new cities were making the Poor Law system unworkable. Costs rose and local and national government had new expenses to pay for basic education, support charitable hospitals, public health works and so on.

The effect of war
The first attempt to create a more comprehensive welfare state was spurred on by the war in South Africa (The Boer War). The British army found that the majority of its working class recruits were so unhealthy they were not fit for military service. Something had to be done.

Under the 1906–1911 Liberal government, a whole host of measures were enacted:
• the first state pensions for the poor

• the first schemes to give access to GPs for the poor

• providing milk for children in schools.

In the years leading up to the Second World War, the power of organised labour through the Trade Union movement, along with supporters from other parts of UK society, began to argue for the development of more universal services that would cover the whole population, and for the comprehensive reorganisation of social security, health services and education.

GURU TIP
Be alert to the limits of systems, such as welfare states. Things are very rarely clear cut and AS General Studies encourages you to think about the whole range of ideas.

Welfare states are an excellent example of how value systems and political ideologies practically shape the instituions we live with. Check out more on value systems on pages 86–89.

Society, politics and the economy

After the war: a new Welfare State

Surviving and winning the Second World War required an extraordinary collective national effort. It was clear from the early years of the war that there would need to be some kind of social pay-off for the majority of the population, and no return to the biting poverty and inequality of the 1930s during the great economic depression: a new Welfare State.

The National Health Service

Although there were many voices and many forces at work in shaping the new Welfare State, the key text of the era was written by Sir William Beveridge, a career civil servant. His 1942 White Paper on social insurance presented a vision of the post-War Welfare State and many of its practical details. This was combined with the wartime 1944 Education Act and plans were drawn up for the National Health Service (NHS). However, for these plans to be put into action required the election to power in the 1945 General Election of the first majority Labour government in the UK, under Clement Atlee.

This Labour government (1945-51), building on the old order, shifted the UK Welfare State towards a much more social democratic style:

- there was State provision of housing through local Councils (Council housing).
- The NHS was a truly universal service.
- Social benefits became more widespread and generous.

Although the Conservatives had opposed many of the details of the plans, by the time they returned to government in 1951, they were committed to retaining all the key features of the Welfare State – this was called the 'post-war consensus'.

The Welfare State today

The UK Welfare State has undergone significant reform in the last twenty years. Under the Conservatives, between 1979 and 1997 there was a concerted attempt to reduce the role of the public sector, and increase that of the voluntary and private sectors in welfare provision. For example, nearly all Council housing was passed to the control of voluntary housing associations. There have also been significant internal reforms of health and education, with the creation of the internal market in the NHS (see page 104) and the National Curriculum in education.

Under the Labour government (1997 –), these reforms have generally been maintained and adapted, but with greater efforts to find more money for investment in key services. Nonetheless, significant debate and problems remain, these include:

- **Expectation and capacity.** As people get richer they expect better and better services but are not always willing to pay the taxes that would fund them.
- **Demographics.** The UK is an ageing society and older people consume more welfare services (pensions, health care etc.) than the young or middle-aged. As the number of workers paying tax declines relative to the number of retired people, the amount each person must pay towards maintaining the Welfare State increases.
- **Setting targets.** The Labour government has used target setting, such as reducing waiting lists as a way of raising the performance of NHS hospitals. This has led to other targets and priorities being neglected. Shorter waiting list might mean a quicker turnover of patients through a hospital and more readmissions for post-operative problems.

A White Paper is an official statement of government policy, presented to the Houses of Parliament.

GURU TIP
Something like: It's worth learning and using some terms, such as 'post-war consensus', as long as you can use them correctly in context. They show examiners that you have been reading about the subject and know some of the 'shorthand' expressions people use to talk about it.

Assessing the performance of the Welfare State

There have been many debates on the performance of the UK Welfare State since the Second World War. Here are some of the key things different groups have said:

Social Democratic supporters of the Welfare State:

- despite its faults, it has made significant progress in improving the very worst of poverty and deprivation.

- it provides an acceptable safety net for the poor

- it provides unequalled standards of health and education for a mass public

Liberal critics of the Welfare State:

- the public sector is an inefficient provider of welfare services. With no market and no competition there has been too little incentive for efficiency and development of the Welfare State.

- with no possibility of the services being run by competitors, there's no threat to inefficient providers, and little opportunity for consumers to influence the service they receive.

- overall, the cost of the Welfare State is too high, requiring levels of taxation that are harmful to the economy as a whole, as well as being an unfair burden to wage earners.

Socialist critics of the Welfare State:

- that it has been ungenerous to the very poorest. It relies on means-testing, and the stigma and shame that come from applying for these kinds of benefits means many don't claim – a large number of pensioners entitled to income support do not claim it, for example

- many of the Welfare State's biggest expenditures benefit the rich more than the poor. Higher education, for example, has primarily been used by those at the top of the socio-economic scale.

Feminist Critics of the Welfare State:

- the UK Welfare State was created at a time when women did not work and would be expected to rely upon a male partner for income, pensions and so on. For much of the post-war era, women were excluded from many benefits.

- the failure of the Welfare State to consider childcare a service they should provide has helped exclude women from the labour market, or hinder their development through a career.

There is another section in this book that looks at the reforms of the NHS. See pages 102–105.

> **GURU TIP**
> In AS level General Studies it is important to show that you can see an issue from many different points of view and identify their ideological origins, in other words, which groups of people said them.

Society, politics and the economy

The National Health Service (NHS)

The NHS is now over fifty years old, but it has not always been there. Before 1948, the provision of health care in the UK was a patchwork and confusing business.

There were a great many voluntary hospitals, established by churches and other charitable foundations in the 18th and 19th Century. They provided services on a very variable basis: free to some and charging others. THeir sources of finance were equally mixed with some money from charitable sources, some money from the government. General Practioners (GPs) were a mixture of public and private provision, with most families having to pay to use GP services. For the very poor, the 1906-1911 Liberal government had created insurance schemes for some medical care, and many communities created their own co-operatives and friendly societies to fund health care.

Not surprisingly, there were considerable variations in health amongst different social groups and in different parts of the country. Many hospitals teetered on the brink of bankruptcy as 19th Century charitable funds could not meet 20th Century medical needs and governments had been unwilling to close the gap. Organised planning of services and co-operation between different parts of the health service were impossible because there were so many different agencies and institutions with different concerns, providing health care. So, in the years after the First World War, there was a growing call for the creation of a single, unified National Health Service that would provide care on the basis of need rather than ability to pay. Support came from civil servants, doctors and nurses, Trade Unions and politicians.

The creation of the NHS

In 1945, the first majority Labour government was elected under Prime Minister, Clement Atlee. The Secretary of State for Health was Aneurin Bevan, the star of the left wing of the Labour party at the time. Bevan is often seen as the creator of the NHS, but his great achievement was not inventing the idea of the NHS, but taking ideas that already existed and making them politically possible.

Bevan's key opponents were hospital consultants who feared a loss of income and status under the new regime. Bevan famously remarked that his strategy was to 'stuff their mouths with gold'. He bought off the consultants' opposition to the NHS by allowing them to continue to practise privately in a small, but potentially lucrative, private sector. In addition, hospital medicine and senior doctors retained very considerable power and autonomy over how health services operated.

Established in 1948, the NHS, under the direction of the Ministry of Health, was split into three areas:
- hospital medicine
- primary care - mainly GPs
- other local services and public health, mostly under the control of local councils.

Treatment was to be provided to all, free at the point of use (the hospital, surgery etc). In these respects, the NHS did mark a fundamental revolution in health care in the UK and was the most social democratic element of the new Welfare State established between 1945 and 1951.

GURU TIP

Dates, such as the establishment of the NHS in 1948, are important in showing examiners that you have a grasp of the basics. Note the key ones and learn them.

Structural problems of the NHS

The structure of the NHS, laid down between 1945 and 1951 (see diagram below), also created problems that the NHS has spent fifty years struggling with.

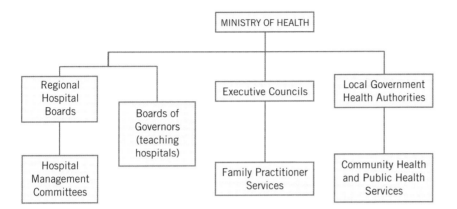

GURU TIP
Diagrams can be very useful and are a concise way of representing the institutional structures. Look out for other examples and use them.

- the focus in the NHS has mainly been on curing illness rather than preventing it. The high status of acute hospital medicine, and the separation of public health from the mainstream NHS, has meant that little progress was made in preventing illness and encouraging public behaviour that would improve people's health.

- Partly because of the priorities mentioned above, the NHS had become more and more expensive. Another factor is that the relative age of the population has increased. There are more older people, who are more expensive to look after. Also, the costs of new technologies, new services and meeting the expectations of a more health-conscious public have risen. At the same time, there have been few incentives for hospitals and doctors to become more efficient and cost conscious.

- A similar imbalance has existed in the relative status and funding of hospital medicine and health care in local communities – GPs, health visitors etc. Hospitals, which tend to deal with people after they have become seriously ill, have received far more money than GPs, who try to keep people generally healthy, and out of hospitals.

- Although the NHS has been available universally, serious inequalities still exist. The NHS inherited some of these: some areas were over-provided with hospitals and others had very few or very old hospitals, for instance. Similarly, richer areas tended to attract more and better GP surgeries, while poor areas were often served by single-doctor practices, providing a narrower range of services. As NHS budgets tended to fund existing services before money was found for new services, the gaps became wider in some areas.

- The structure of the NHS meant that doctors controlled which services were provided. Managers adjusted budgets and spending to match those priorities. It became difficult for governments and managers to shift these priorities and practices, even where it was clear that there would be public benefit from doing so.

Other problems you might want to think about include:

- Does the NHS make space for alternative therapies and medicines?

- Can the NHS continue to attract enough nursing staff on its current budget?

Society, politics and the economy

What political ideologies do you think have helped stage these reforms?

You might find it useful to look at the section on political ideologies values.

Reforms and developments

In the 1960s and 1970s, several attempts were made to reform the NHS. New budget systems channelled extra money to poorer regions. New administrative structures and planning systems were created in 1974 to integrate the different wings of the NHS. The most extensive reform to the NHS was by the Conservative government in 1991: the formation of an internal market. To form an internal market, you have to separate out the purchasers and the providers of health services.

The **purchasers** were the local health authorities, independent, fund-holding GPs, local groups of GPs, and other primary health workers. All of these receive a budget from the government and must plan what services they want to provide. They are then free to buy those services from whichever provider (see below) they choose.

The **providers** of health services are primarily hospital trusts – the legal forms taken by the old hospitals, previously managed by health authorities. There are also local health trusts, more distant health trusts, private sector providers, other voluntary organisations, and so on.

It was argued that the internal market would improve the NHS by:

- putting more planning and decision-making about health services in the hands of managers and local health authorities rather than doctors. This should have placed public interests above more narrow, sectional interests

- providing incentives for purchasers to seek out the best value services, and for providers to think more carefully about their services and costs. Choice and competition should lead to increased efficientcy and better services.

Although the subsequent Labour government has adapted those reforms, many elements of them are still in place The consequences of the internal market are still emerging, but a number of key points to remember are:

Cons	Pros
• The promise of competition has not always worked as, often, there is only one provider that they can realistically purchase services from. • The cost of running the new service, managing and monitoring contracts etc. has been very high, and many efficiency gains have been eroded by greater administrative costs.	• The new system, which has forced all health providers to cost their services, has exposed good and bad practice in the system, and put pressure on poor performers to change and improve. • It has also given more power and resources to local health care providers who often have a better understanding of the need for different types of service.

GURU TIP

Think about the problems involved. What's the point of buying hip replacements in Glasgow for patients in Cornwall?

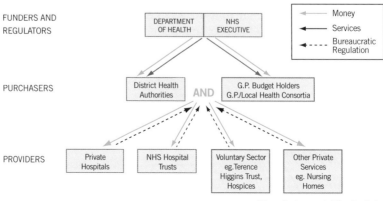

The Internal Market in the NHS

The NHS today: some current debates

Do we spend enough on health? Some people argue that, regardless of efficiency savings and new structures, the NHS just needs more money. Take a look at the table below to see how much of the UK's national income is spent on health compared to other Western countries.

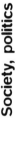

Society, politics and the economy

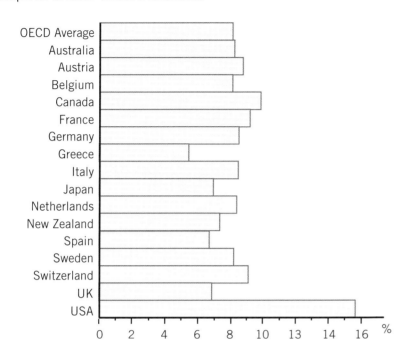

Spending on Health (% of GDP): International Comparisons

The role of the private sector: some people claim that politicians will never persuade the public to pay enough in taxes to fund the kind of NHS that they expect. However, it may be possible to persuade more people to invest in private treatment, reducing the burden on the rest of the NHS. Others say that this would encourage more and more people to opt out of the NHS and, eventually, to refuse to pay taxes on top of their health insurance to fund an NHS for the poor.

Changing behaviour: how can everyone become healthier and avoid illness by changing the way they live - exercising more, smoking less, eating better? Some people say that more should be done to create a cleaner, more healthy environment, and to diminish the risks of work-related accidents and stresses.

Alternative therapies: There has been an enormous growth in the use of alternative therapies. Simultaneous pathic confidence in the assumptions and appriach of conventional medicine has fallen. Should alternative therapies be available on the NHS?

Law and ethics

The topic of the law and its relationship to moral and ethical questions crops up a lot in AS General Studies. The kinds of questions these terms raise include:

- Does the law actually represent the moral beliefs of the public? If not, why not?

- Is it right to disobey the law under certain circumstances. If so, which laws and which circumstances?

Below, you can begin to explore these questions. There is another section in this book that looks at the nature of ethical and value systems. See the section on the Values in Society, page 86.

GURU TIP
In AS General Studies, you need to be a sceptic. Whatever your final answer, a questioning attitude to problems will be recognised.

What is a crime?

One very simple definition of a crime is that it is an action that breaks the law of the land.

To put the legal definition of crime more formally: crimes are acts that are codified in law; in the case of our society, a law that has been created, policed and enforced by the UK State (the police, the criminal justice system, Parliament, the Home Office etc.)

Another place to look for a definition is in a dictionary. The Oxford English Dictionary (OED) sees things in a more complex light. Its definition of a crime is:

> An Act punishable by law, as being forbidden by statute or injurious to the public welfare. . . An evil or injurious act; an offence, sin; esp. of a grave character

This definition begs a whole host of questions:
- Does the law cover all acts that are injurious to the public welfare? Does that include disastrous economic decisions taken by a government?
- Does the law forbid all the sins of the world? For an orthodox Muslim, consuming alcohol is a sin, but it is not codified by UK law.
- Is it always against the law, always an evil act, to take another life? What about in wartime or assisting euthanasia?

These problems arise because the OED definition of crime combines two ways of thinking about law and ethics. On the one hand it adopts the legal definition of crime, explained above. On the other hand, crimes are acts which can offend against a set of norms, a value system or moral framework – this is the normative definition of crime.

Law and ethics

What other examples can you think of where value systems and the law might come into conflict? What happens? There are lots of examples you could come up with, but one example worth dwelling on is civil disobedience - organised, but illegal, forms of collective protest.

Examples of civil disobedience include:
- many of the actions taken by the suffragette movement in pursuit of votes for women
- the sit-downs and blockades organised by the civil rights movement in the USA in the 1960s, seeking to end segregation and systematic discrimination by race
- The anti-nuclear weapons protest of the 1980s, where protesters attacked and occupied military bases.

The key things for you to think about are what are the arguments that might justify this kind of action and what are the arguments against?

GURU TIP

Sometimes it is worth your while learning some basic definitions - like the two definitions of crime to use in your essays. It might even be worth learning the OED quote as it illustrates a complex problem very simply.

Society, politics and the economy

Arguments for civil disobedience:	Arguments against civil disobedience:
• The validity of a law is determined by the circumstances under which it was made. If a law was made under a system that excludes parts of a society, the excluded have a right to reject the moral worth of that law. This argument would apply to the exclusion of women from the franchise (vote) by a system that did not include any women.	• The preservation of the law, and the rule of law rather than the rule of who can shout loudest is itself a fundamental precondition of a good society. This is challenged at a society's peril.
• The validity of a law can be challenged morally where individuals believe that a greater moral bad is being sustained or perpetrated. This would be the argument that nuclear protestors would draw upon.	• There are limits to the degree to which any protest can justifiably disrupt other people's lives. Those who are not involved in a conflict over the law have a right to be left undisturbed and pursue their everyday life.

GURU TIP

Research the following famous controversial cases to add weight to your death penalty arguments:
- James Hanratty
- Ruth Ellis
- Derek Bentley.

A recent example of a debate, revolves around the actions of animal rights movement, in the UK. The radical wing of the movement has taken illegal action against companies that conduct animal experiments. The action was not only taken against the companies, but against the employees, shareholders and banks. The action included various types of harrassment, property damage to laboratories and release of animals. The companies and their supporters argue that they are conducting legitimate business, support many jobs and livelihoods and in the case of medical research, make a significant contribution to human health. The protestors argue that the moral case against harming animals is so strong that illegal action is justified. What do you think? Do you think the direction of medical research should be decided in this kind of conflict? Does cruelty demand an extreme reaction?

Crime: the death penalty

The debate over the abolition of the death penalty continues to raise questions about how legitimate it is for punishing certain crimes and deterring others. It is a moral and emotional issue and you will need to understand the arguments from both sides in order to tackle a question about whether it is an effective deterrent or used purely as an act of retribution.

GURU TIP
Debate the advantages and disadvantages of the death penalty, ensuring that everyone voices their opinions fairly and coherently. Listen carefully and make sure that your arguments respond to what a fellow student has said.

KEY SKILLS C3.1a

The death penalty in England

- **1530–1630**: 70 000 people were hanged in England.
- **1772**: more than 350 capital crimes (offences that carry the death penalty) existed in Britain.
- **Early nineteenth century**: social and political reforms drastically reduced the use of the death penalty.
- **1861**: the number of capital crimes had been reduced to four: murder, treason, arson in dock yards and piracy on the high seas.
- **1945–1958**: a series of hangings had doubt cast over the convictions.
- This public disquiet led to the **1957 Homicide Act**. Murder still carried the death penalty but defences of diminished responsibility and provocation were introduced.
- **1962**: the hanging of James Hanratty 'the A6 murderer' reignited the debate about abolishing capital punishment. Many people believed Hanratty was innocent, including Janet Gregsten, the widow of his alleged victim, who requested a posthumous pardon.
- **1964**: the last executions of two men convicted of murder took place.
- **1965**: a bill abolishing the death penalty was passed on a five-year experimental basis.
- **1969**: the abolition was made permanent for all crimes except treason and piracy with violence.
- **1990**: a move to reintroduce the death penalty for common crimes was defeated in the House of Commons by 367 votes to 182.
- **2000**: there have been renewed requests to exhume the body of James Hanratty to prove, forensically, that he was innocent.

'There is no crime more antithetical to the idea of a civil society of free individuals than murder. It is therefore altogether fitting that the people in their collective moral capacity should decree that those who deliberately take a life shall pay with their own.'

G L McDowell, Professor of American Studies, University of London

Arguments in favour of the death penalty

Eighty-seven countries (source: Amnesty International) still retain the death penalty so there is clearly plenty of belief in it. Here are some of the arguments in favour of the death penalty for you to think about. As you read through them, imagine that you have to give a speech in favour of the death penalty. How could you develop these points?

- Surveys conducted by Amnesty International into American attitudes towards the death penalty show that 3 out of every 4 people support it. As crime rates escalate in the US, opposition to the death penalty is now seen by many as being 'soft' on crime.
- In Britain, supporters favour a return to capital punishment for premeditated murder because of the continual rise in the murder rate since it was abolished.
- The moral argument suggests that law must carry a sanction that will reflect the moral seriousness of an offence and this would enable people to understand with certainty what was just and unjust. Certain acts must be seen as unacceptable and those who commit them should forfeit their right to live in a civilised society.
- The most common argument in support of the death penalty is deterrence: it dissuades other people from committing the same kind of crime.

Arguments against the death penalty

Again, here is a list of arguments against the death penalty. Prepare your speech against the death penalty then present your findings to a friend. Encourage them to find flaws in your arguments. This will help you both develop your viewpoints and test your strength of opinion.

GURU TIP
Look at the Amnesty International website on www.amnesty.org/ to find out more information on the death penalty.

- Crimes are not usually committed in a rational frame of mind, weighing up the consequences – they are most often committed when extreme emotion overcomes reason, or under the influence of drugs or alcohol. Criminals can often be highly unstable or mentally ill. Therefore, in such cases, fear of the death penalty is unlikely to deter.

- If the death penalty worked more effectively than other punishments you would think that countries with the death penalty for a particular crime would have a lower crime rate than those which do not, but this is not true. For example, Britain's murder rate is 14 times less than America's.

- The death penalty clearly contravenes the United Nations Universal Declaration of Human Rights – it denies the right to life and the right not to be tortured or subjected to any cruel, inhuman or degrading punishment.

- US researchers have estimated that 350 innocent people have been wrongfully convicted of murder this century. For 23 of the prisoners, the evidence establishing their innocence appeared after they had been executed.

- Numerous studies have failed to establish any conclusive links between the reintroduction of the death penalty and a drop in crime rates.

- Roger Hood, the director of the Criminological Research Centre at Oxford University, found in a survey carried out for the United Nations that there is no scientific proof that 'executions have a greater deterrent effect than life imprisonment.'

'Turn on the juice, fry him, and don't let's hear his name again'.
WSG radio show host Neal Boortz
on the execution of Nicholas Ingram in Georgia, 1995

'I feel morally and intellectually obligated to concede that the death penalty experiment has failed . . . [it] remains fraught with arbitrariness, discrimination, caprice and mistake.'
US Supreme Court Justice, Harry A. Blackmun

'No country which resorts to legalised murder can claim to be truly civilised'.
Judith Ward, wrongly convicted for murder in 1974

'The fruit of my experience has this bitter after-taste: that I do not believe that any one of the hundreds of executions I carried out has in any way acted as a deterrent against future murder. Capital punishment in my view achieved nothing except revenge.'
Albert Pierrepoint, Britain's hangman for 9 years

'Electrocution produces, 'visible destructive effects as the body's internal organs are burned; the prisoner often leaps forward against the restraining straps when the switch is thrown; the body changes colour; the flesh swells and may even catch fire; the prisoner may defecate, urinate or vomit blood. Witnesses always report that there is a smell of burning flesh.'
Amnesty International USA Death Penalty Briefing 1987

Society, politics and the economy

Crime: prison

Every year, government statistics report that crime figures have risen or fallen by publishing numbers showing how many incidents have been recorded. Statistics notoriously never tell the whole story because many crimes, approximately half the number committed, remain unreported, and around a quarter do not get recorded by the police. The annual number of crimes is therefore even larger than is shown in the statistics.

What is statistically indisputable, however, is the fact that the number of crimes recorded by the police in Britain has gradually increased from the 1950s, when there were less than half a million crimes recorded annually, to the 1990s where there are over five and a quarter million crimes recorded annually. Several theories attempt to explain this increase in crime:

- The growth of youth culture since the post war years has made adolescents a separate group in society, reducing the influence of adults on their behaviour, increasing the power of their peer group and therefore encouraging more anti-social or criminal behaviour.

- Late twentieth-century capitalism has created a society based on individualism, materialism and greed.

- More people are now prepared to report crimes.

As a result of this increase in crime, the prison population is at an all time high. The question you need to ask yourself is whether a custodial sentence is an effective way of punishing criminals or whether a wider variety of alternative strategies need to be implemented to stem the rise in crime.

Aims of punishment

Think about what you believe a punishment for crime should achieve.

- Should it humiliate the criminal in order to deter others from committing the same crime?

- Should it rehabilitate criminals in order to help prevent them from committing crime in the future?

- The British Humanist Association believe that the following objectives should inform the punishment of criminals. How far do you agree with them? How far does a prison sentence go towards fulfilling these objectives?

1. The punishment should reflect moral condemnation of the crime.

2. It should deter others from committing similar offences.

3. It should protect society if the offender is liable to repeat the offence.

4. It should seek to reform and rehabilitate the offender.

5. It should allow the offender where possible to give some benefit to society or to those injured by the crime.

6. It should not of itself lead to failure of justice nor inflict damage on society.

Does prison work?

From the official point of view, the functions of a prison sentence address the BHA's recommendations to:

- reform
- rehabilitate
- protect society
- deter potential criminals
- punish.

Opponents of prison sentences argue the following:

- All a prison sentence does is punish by depriving a criminal of their liberty.

- If prisons worked to deter crime, jails would empty and crime would fall.

- Prisons are ineffective and costly both in human and financial terms. Home Office research suggests that prison works minimally. You get only a 1% reduction in crime for every extra 25% rise in the prison population and prisoners cost approximately £25 000 a year to maintain.

- Statistics show that the rate of reoffending among ex-prisoners is extremely high, therefore prison fails to deter or rehabilitate.

- Prisons do not protect society because prisoners typically learn from each other how to be better criminals.

So what alternative strategies could be put in place to complement or replace prison?

Alternatives to prison

The following strategies are just a few suggestions for alternative means of dealing with crime:

- More projects that will rehabilitate the offender and allow them to give some benefit to society or the victims of their crime, could be implemented. For example, the process of mediation, where criminals must meet with their victims, allows offenders to face up to what they have done, lets them apologise and perhaps repair the damage. This is coupled with an action plan that addresses the offending causes of the behaviour.

- Many researchers point to neglect and child-abuse as being a prime cause of crime in later life. One American programme gave a year's intensive teaching to pre-schoolers from high-risk families in Detroit for a few hours a day. The children are now 31 and compared to others from identical backgrounds are five times less likely to offend.

- In America, a large number of young men identified in infancy as being high crime risks were put into Head Start employment programmes and in some cities the effectiveness of those schemes has resulted in a reduction of crime.

Consequently, you could argue that government funding needs to concentrate less on trying to catch and incarcerate a small percentage of criminals and more on addressing why more criminals continue to offend: lack of skill, limited employment opportunities, despair at having no future, drugs. If funds were used to tackle the causes, e.g. offering intensive assistance to high-risk families and helping schools deal with disaffected, anti-social children, then crime rates would surely drop in the long term.

Discuss whether you think that alternatives to prison offer viable options or do you believe that custodial sentences play a necessary role in controlling crime in this country.

GURU TIP
Make a list of statutory prison sentences to keep it clear in your mind.

KEY SKILLS
Search for and select appropriate information to make a list of statutory prison sentences using IT resources, such as the Internet or CD ROMs.

GURU TIP
Make up a list of alternative sentencing to prison to keep it clear in your mind.

Society, politics and the economy

The European Union

Useful terms
CAP – common agricultural policy to stabilise agricultural markets in the EU by fixing agricultural products at a maximum price.

common market – group of countries exercising free trade and a common external tariff.

single European market – EU agreement to remove trade barriers

excise duties – tax on alcohol, fuel, tobacco and betting.

With the imminent introduction of the Euro, the expansion of its Member States and the UK's rejection of EMU, the European Union is a popular choice of examination question in both essay or multiple choice forms. Again, you will be best placed to tackle an essay if you have prior knowledge of the subject and keep up with the news (which you should be doing as a matter of course!) which is a great source of information on European issues. This section also complements the globalisation section and it would therefore be profitable to study these two sections together. As you do so, try to think about whether the UK is right to maintain its stance against total European integration, or whether this way of thinking completely defeats the objectives behind the EU?

The European Union is the political and economic alliance of a number of European countries who share responsibility in the following areas:
- the single market
- monetary policy
- economic and social cohesion
- foreign and security policy
- employment policy
- environmental protection
- foreign and defence policy
- the creation of an area of freedom and justice.

Since 1995, the EU has had 15 Member States:
- the original six members who joined in 1957 were Belgium, France, West Germany, Italy, Luxembourg, and the Netherlands
- followed by the UK, Denmark and the Republic of Ireland in 1973
- Greece in 1981
- Spain and Portugal in 1986
- Austria, Finland and Sweden in 1995.
- Countries awaiting the possibility of full EU membership are the Czech Republic, Slovenia, Hungary, Poland and Estonia.

The EU is built around the idea of a 'common market' which aims to:
- encourage and expand trade between its member countries
- abolish restrictive trading practices
- encourage free movement of capital and labour within the EU
- set a common tariff on goods and services imported outside of the union
- establish a closer union between European people.

Advantages to businesses within the EU
- The abolition of trade barriers allows businesses to shop around Europewide for the best deals on, for example, materials and production costs
- They are protected from competition by companies outside the common market
- Increased competition between businesses in the common market could act as an incentive to increase efficiency and standards
- The marketplace has a potential 370 million plus consumers.

Disadvantages to businesses within the EU

- Imported goods and services from outside the EU are more expensive because of the common external tariff

- The protection from competition from external countries may reduce the incentive for companies to increase efficiency

- Companies may incur extra costs in selling their products in other EU countries

- Increased competition from other EU countries may force some smaller domestic producers out of business.

The single European currency

The latest step in European economic integration is European Monetary Union (EMU). Eleven Member States joined in 1999 and fixed their exchange rates so that they could not move at all against each other. The exchange rate is the price of one currency in relation to another. If you have travelled abroad and changed any English money into foreign currency, you will have seen, for example, that one pound may be the equivalent of ten French Francs. On 1 January 2002, Euro notes and coins will become the legal tender of these countries and they will therefore share a single currency which will later replace their national currencies.

Supporters of the single European currency believe that these fixed exchange rates will have the following desirable effects:

- It will be clear to see exactly how much things cost in different countries because the prices will all be shown in Euros

- There will be few costs incurred by changing from one currency to another to buy foreign goods and services

- Fixed exchange rates means that prices within the 'Euro-zone' will not be prone to fluctuations which suddenly increase the price of foreign goods and services

- Fixed exchange rates will be maintained by controlling interest rates, which will in turn help to keep inflation low.

Opponents of the single European currency, such as the UK and Denmark, believe that it would bring the following disadvantages:

- The economies of the member countries of the EU are too different for them to converge. Germany, for example, is economically much stronger than Greece and it is therefore unrealistic to expect a system of tighter economic integration to work

- Training staff in the use of the new currency and re-pricing products will incur great costs

- National governments will inevitably loose some of their power by participating in it, as many decisions over economic affairs would be taken by EU institutions. UK opponents believe that this may not always suit the UK and businesses may suffer as a consequence.

GURU TIP

Divide a sheet of paper and make a list of the advantages and disadvantages of total European integration. This will help you see more clearly where you stand in the debate.

Acts and treaties

The Treaty of Rome (1957) – signed by the original 6 countries to focus on the creation of a common market and economic integration.

The Single European Act (1987) – aimed to remove trade barriers and create a single European market by 1992.

The Maastricht Treaty (1992) – terms for closer economic and political co-operation between the member countries.

The Treaty of Amsterdam (1997) – created political and institutional conditions so the EU could tackle future challenges, such as globalisation, crime and ecological problems.

The European Monetary Union (1999) was formed involving 11 EU members (excluding the UK)

Society, politics and the economy

Globalisation

Questions on economics and trade are best tackled by those studying these areas. This summary of globalisation will enable you to access the main points and help you decide what factors have contributed to its growth, any advantages or disadvantages globalisation has brought and whether globalisation means westernisation.

What is globalisation?

Globalisation is the process of enabling businesses, and financial and investment markets to operate internationally. You could say that globalisation integrates national economies into a single global economy and consequently large businesses look at succeeding on the world market instead of only in their country of origin.

An example of a company that operates on the world market is Nike, which markets its sportswear across the globe. It is a brand that is easy to recognise and works alongside businesses in other countries who manufacture, distribute and sell Nike products. Nike is able to operate on such a large scale because of globalisation.

Why has globalisation grown?

- Technology – more powerful computers and communications technology, such as the Internet, have revolutionised the transfer and acquisition of data.
- Transportation – the cost of transportation and communication has fallen dramatically over the years.
- Deregulation – many businesses across the world became privatised throughout the 1980s and 1990s, which meant that previously state-owned monopolies could then compete on the global market.
- Liberalisation of trade – trade barriers, tariffs and trading restrictions have been reduced which has helped less wealthy countries to compete globally.
- Consumer tastes – these have changed as many consumers across the world are more likely to buy foreign products, such as cars, than ever before.
- Emerging markets and competitions – previously poor countries, such as some former communist countries or those just opening up to tourism, have become wealthy enough to compete in the world market.

This table contains a few terms that you should familiariase yourself with:

• **Multinational businesses**	Large companies that operate in several (or more) countries, such as Coca Cola.
• **Market**	The trading or selling opportunities provided by a particular group of people, such as the foreign market.
• **Hypercompetition**	The disruption of existing markets by flexible, fast-moving businesses.
• **World Trade Organisation**	An organisation which seeks to promote free trade between nations and monitors world trade.
• **Group of Seven (G7) or G8 countries**	The 7 leading industrial countries – Canada, France, Germany, Italy, Japan, US and UK (and Russia when it is referred to as G8) who generate over two-thirds of the world's total output and aim to devote a joint strategy to promote growth in the world economy.
• **Balance of payments**	Transactions between one country and the rest of the world over a given period of time.

Features of globalisation:

- international trade – this has more than doubled over the past two decades.
- multinational businesses – which have rapidly spread throughout the world over the last 50 years.
- global business strategies – many businesses now think globally, not nationally, about their strategies.
- the global city – cities growing up around the world in different countries which are exhibiting the same traits, cultivating the same consumer habits and pastimes and beginning to look similar.

Effects of globalisation

Globalisation affects different companies in different ways: larger businesses may be forced to undergo dramatic changes, while small businesses, serving local communities, may not notice the effects of globalisation. Likewise, some businesses will thrive on the global markets while others will suffer. As you read through the effects of globalisation, try to think of examples of businesses that have either gained or lost out because of the effects of globalisation.

- **Competition** – increases on a global market for several reasons. Foreign competition enters markets previously served, mainly or exclusively, by domestic businesses.
- **Deregulation** – businesses that had virtually no competition, must compete now.
- **Innovation** – new innovative companies will be able to compete with established heavyweights who had dominated the market.
- **Consumer expectations and tastes** – more competition means that businesses must now be more sensitive to consumer demands than ever before. They must be more competitive over quality and price and produce a greater choice of products to satisfy consumers' demands.
- **Economies of scale** – larger businesses with large-scale operations can produce things more economically, which will be of benefit to themselves and the consumer.
- **Location** – global businesses can choose the best location for each of its operations by weighing up advantages and disadvantages. For example, some countries, such as China, are cheaper to manufacture in than others.
- **Mergers and joint ventures** – businesses can now merge or join with businesses in other countries to distribute their goods or services to a global market more easily.

Multinationals

Advantages of creating a multinational company:	Disadvantages of creating a multinational company:
• they create jobs and can therefore improve the standard of living in poorer countries • they can benefit the balance of payments if the products are sold abroad • they can introduce new technology and production processes in countries that may lack technical expertise • they can finance projects to protect the environment in that country.	• if they shift production facilities they can cause mass unemployment • locals may be employed as low-skill labourers as managers are drafted in from other countries • some safety measures used by multinational companies in developing countries are in doubt • they can avoid strict government controls giving them an unfair advantage over the market.

KEY SKILLS
Using different sources, research as many effects of globalisation that you can find, perhaps email your Business Studies department for help, and present your findings using automated routines such as spreadsheets, bar and pie charts.

Society, politics and the economy

The poverty gap

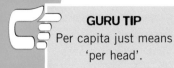
GURU TIP
Per capita just means
'per head'.

The 'poverty gap' refers to the difference in wealth between the richer and poorer countries across the world. You can measure wealth and poverty in lots of different ways. One way is to look at the GDP (Gross Domestic Product) of countries – that's the money exchanged for all the goods and services in a country's economy in a single year. If you divide that total by the population, you get GDP per capita. Another way is to look at what people (rather than companies or governments) actually consume. Both ways are shown in the tables below.

Note that the tables divide the populations of the world into three groups.

- 20% live in high-income countries: Western Europe, North America, Australia, Japan, South Korea and Singapore.

- 20% live in low-income countries: nearly all in sub-Saharan Africa and southern Asian societies.

- 60% live in middle income countries: Latin America, the Caribbean, North Africa and the middle East, and the ex-Soviet states.

Sometimes the richest countries are referred to collectively as the North and the rest as the South. Although the terms are not geographically accurate, they are a useful shorthand.

Vocabulary
GDP
GDP per capita
north and south
Empire colonialism
Industrial revolution.

	Total (Millions US$)	Per Capita (US$)		Total (Millions US$)	Per Capita (US$)
World	27 687 323	4 880	Low income	1 381 813	430
Africa	412 160	758	Middle Income	3 797 316	2 390
UK	1 094 734	18 700	High income	22 508 193	24 930

Gross National Product estimates 1995

Consumption share of the richest 20%

Middle 60%

Poorest 60%

Total consumption expenditure · Cars · Paper · Telephone connections · Electricity · Total energy · Meat · Fish · Cereals

20% share

60% share

20% share

Shares of world consumption 1995

Looking at the tables, you may ask yourself some questions:
- Why are nearly all the richest societies in the world either in Western Europe or in societies colonised (settled) by Western Europeans?
- Why have some East Asian societies, such as Japan and South Korea, become equally prosperous?
- Why is the most serious poverty concentrated in sub-Saharan Africa and southern Asia?

Some answers to these questions are suggested on the next three pages.

Empire and colonialism

If the data in the tables on page 108 had been gathered for the world in the 15th Century, they would have looked very different. The world as a whole was significantly poorer, but the geographical spread of wealth and poverty would have been very different, too.

- The Americas and Australia would have been amongst the poorest societies

- Africa would have boasted wealthy empires in the South and the West and rich trading cities on its East Coast.

- The Chinese and Islamic empires would have been amongst the richest, and the great imperial domains of Southern Asia would have been close behind.

- Europe would have been, by comparison, a rather poor place on the western edge of the great Eurasian landmass.

Here is how the colonisation of the rest of the world by European countries began to change the distribution of wealth.

- . In the 16th Century, European countries began to colonise the Americas and Australasia. Indigenous (native) societies were defeated by force, but also by European diseases. Indigenous populations were effectively replaced by European settlers and their descendants.

> Measles and the common cold killed up to 90% of local populations within a generation of settlers arriving.

- European empires controlled Southern and South Eastern Asia politically, although they did not colonise here. By the early 20th Century, nearly all of Africa and the Middle East were in a similar position. China, though never colonised, was economically controlled by Europe.

- Beginning in the late 18th Century in Britain, European societies and North America experienced industrial revolutions. The combination of new technologies, new investments and increasing productivity massively expanded their economic output and wealth.

- Before the Second World War, only uncolonised Japan was able to start a successful industrial revolution and grow rapidly in wealth.

So, very simply, the origins of the world's current rich and poor can be explained by successful industrialisation in the North (including Japan), and late or failed industrialisation in the South. You can find out more about the legacy of colonialism on the South on the next two pages.

GURU TIP
It is always useful to compare social issue across time. Things may not always have been as they are now and if so then it is important to ask why and how things have changed.

Society, politics and the economy

GURU TIP
You can never know too much history for AS General Studies. A great way of learning a lot of history, quickly, is to look at an atlas of world history.

Maps, diagrams and pictures help you remember complex historical processes, far more easily.

The legacy of colonialism

In part, the relative poverty of the South and its failure to develop (see the previous two pages) was a legacy of colonialism. These are some of the reasons why:

- European empires established a strict economic division of labour between the home country and the colonies. The colonies provided cheap raw materials, labour and markets for imperial companies, but did not benefit from the profits.

- The process of colonialism inhibited industrialisation in many societies, for example, the British deliberately destroyed the Egyptian cotton industry

On the other hand, colonisation and empire – in the case of India, for example – accelerated the introduction of the railways, which was an advantage to the colonised country.

Escaping poverty – South Korea

Since the Second World War, all the European empires have either collapsed or steadily retreated, as former colonies became independent - a process called decolonisation. All of these colonies were low-income societies. Why have some of them been able to shift from being low to high-income countries? One example is South Korea.

Korea was a colony of the Japanese Empire from 1910-1945. It then divided in a brutal, costly civil war (1949-53) into communist North Korea and capitalist South Korea. Today, South Korea is easily as wealthy as Spain. The following factors were important in how this came about.

GURU TIP

It is important in General Studies to support general or abstract arguments with some concrete examples.

Political stability	Korean politics has been frozen since the end of the war. Although the country has been divided, the status of the south and its borders was secured by the military presence of America in the country.
Strong state	South Korea had an authoritarian government until the late 1980s. The government exerted a lot of control over what banks and companies did, what money should be invested in, how much workers got paid, and so on, providing a stable environment for business. Resources were concentrated in investment in economic development rather than in wages or personal consumption
Access to investment and technology	The American armed forces spent a huge amount of money during and after the war with Korean companies, and building infrastructure, such as roads and airports. The American presence also provided access to new technologies.

Other societies have made the leap from poor to rich in a similar wary to South Korea: Singapore and Hong Kong, for instance. Some small, Middle Eastern states have risen on the back of huge oil production, though, as Iran and Iraq show, lots of oil is not enough on its own, especially in big countries.

Remaining poor

Lots of societies have been unable to repeat South Korea's performance. Why this is so varies according to country, but some of the following factors are significant.

Legacy of colonialism I	Many states, especially in sub-Saharan Africa were very frail, divided states when they became independent. The borders of many African nations were drawn up for colonial convenience, leaving many pre-imperial African societies split between different states. This also created states that were very diverse religiously, ethnically and politically. Many of the internal conflicts and international wars in Africa over the last twenty years stem from these problem. War is not an environment in which economies can prosper.
Legacy of colonialism II	Even where there has been relative peace, many societies have not possessed the states and administrators that could initiate or guide an industrial revolution. The Imperial adminstrations set up by European powers were designed to keep the peace and extract resources, and little else. Very few African states had access to a body of trained administrators, economists and so on.
Lack of capital and technology	South Korea was able to draw upon capital, investment and technology from the North as well as generating its own. Many of the world's poorest nations have been unable to do so, or have collected significant and crippling debts after early borrowings had been squandered or stolen by local elites.

There is another section in this book that looks at the impact of international debt. See pages 120–122.

It is important to note that the explanations of the poverty gap (above) are all external explanations. What about internal explanations? Consider the case of South Vietnam, which received as much AMerican support as South Korea but never embarked on any serious programme of industrialisation. Compare India, which has a very patchy record of industrialisation with contemporary China, which is udergoing one of the fastest industrial revolutions ever, on its Pacific coast.

Think about the following:

- is authoritarian politics (right wing in South Korea, left-wing in China) better for industrialisation than democratic politics, such as in India?
- however much external support a country has, ruling elites that lose the confidence of their population (South Vietnam) cannot initiate economic development.

GURU TIP

Comparing countries or different examples is an importune way of arguing in AS level. Comparison of successful and unsuccessful industrialisation is a good example of this. Try and use this way of arguing where you can.

What other factors might affect a societies progress of economic growth? What might be the impact of environmental probelms, such as deforestation and desertification?

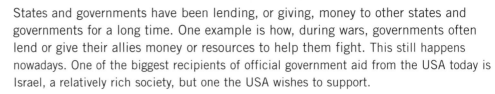
International debt and international aid

States and governments have been lending, or giving, money to other states and governments for a long time. One example is how, during wars, governments often lend or give their allies money or resources to help them fight. This still happens nowadays. One of the biggest recipients of official government aid from the USA today is Israel, a relatively rich society, but one the USA wishes to support.

Governments have also been borrowing money from foreign banks for a long time and, today, all the governments of the world borrow money on the international capital markets. This lending and borrowing leads to a web of debt and aid between the countries of the world. However, when you hear the terms international debt and international aid in a General Studies context, people usually mean the debt and aid passing between the countries of the so-called North and South, the rich and poor societies of the world.

North and South: debt and aid

Although the actual amounts of money involved in the North-South debt and aid flow is quite small in a global context, it has an enormous significance to the poorer countries. Most of today's international debt originated in the 1970s. Between 1973 and 1974 the price of oil quadrupled as OPEC (Organisation of Petroleum Exporting Countries, including Saudi Arabia, Venezuela, Iran and Iraq) controlled oil production to push prices up. As most oil was consumed in the North, and produced in the South, there was a huge flow of money from North to South. Much of that money was placed in Northern banks, which then needed to invest the money to make profits themselves.

Northern economies were going through a recession at the time, so the demand for capital to invest in their own countries was low. The banks found an alternative: the governments of the poor, Southern countries, which were desperate for funds. These countries took on massive borrowing programmes and Northern banks didn't ask too many questions about their ability to repay the loans.

The international debt crisis
While interest rates were low and the market for the South's goods (oil and agricultural cash crops, such as coffee) was doing well, Southern governments were able to pay back the interest. However, in the late 1970s, interest rates began to climb, commodity prices fell, and Southern governments were unable to meet their loan repayments. Matters came to a head in 1982 when Mexico – one of the largest debtors – announced that it was suspending repayments. In effect, the nation was bankrupt.

Panic spread through the world's financial community. Some Northern banks were threatened with collapse. It became clear that the borrowed money had done little good to the economies of the South. Much of it had gone on military expenditure, or had been salted away by corrupt elites (often back into northern, especially Swiss, bank accounts).

International Monetary Fund
Since the crisis, the International Monetary Fund (IMF), which is part of the United Nations, has acted as the last resort for governments, by providing funds to pay off their creditors. But the price of help from the IMF is that countries which receive funds have had to accept Structural Adjustment Programmes (SAPs).

The diagram, below, shows how the international debt crisis is dependent on many factors. Each stage in the diagram is just one example at that stage.

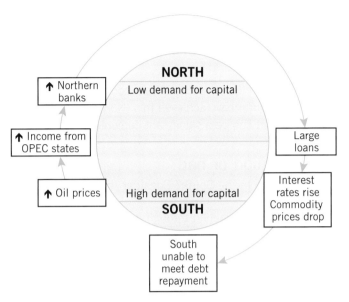

Flow diagram of the international debt crisis

What are Structural Adjustment Programmes?

Broadly, SAPs are a program of economic and social policies designed to ensure that a country has enough foreign currency (usually dollars) to pay its interest charges on borrowing. Exports need to rise and imports fall, and the government must save as much money as it can, paying its bills to the banks before it pays anything else. Policies for achieving this include:

- cutting back on government expenditure on health, education and social services.
- cutting back on expenditure on food subsidies
- cutting government employment
- the sale of national assets and national industries to foreign corporations to raise foreign exchange.
- shifting land-use from small-scale subsistence farming that earns no export income to cash crop production on large farms.

While these policies help in the short term to secure sufficient foreign exchange to pay debts, they have affected the poorest people very badly. They have lost access to services, been forced off the land, and the price of basic foods has risen massively.

In recent years, opinion has steadily turned against SAPs, led by organisations, such as Jubilee 2000. Jubilee 2000 argue that the unpayable debts of the very poorest countries should be written off altogether, as they are stuck in a vicious circle of increasing debt and economic and social problems.

Society, politics and the economy

GURU TIP
Flow diagrams and mind maps can be a useful way of understanding, revising and remembering complex sequences of events. Have a go at drawing up diagrams of your own, on other topics.

Arguments about international aid

International aid is given by many different organisations and can be used for:
- short-term emergencies, such as famines
- long-term investment in infrastructure
- export guarantees – loans for Southern governments to buy goods from Northern companies ('tied aid').

The UN has proposed that Northern nations should contribute 0.7% of their GDP to aid programmes, but only a handful have achieved this (Norway for example). For many nations in the South, the aid can be a significant percentage of their national income.

International aid: good or bad?

Is aid a help or a hindrance to the South? Consider the following arguments:

Problems
- Much aid is channelled through corrupt governments and administrations. Little of it benefits the poorest and most vulnerable
- Aid encourages the dependency of Southern societies on the North
- Aid can distort the free market, propping up inefficient producers
- A lot of aid is tied to the purchase of military (and therefore non-productive) goods from the North.
- Aid programmes can reinforce a negative view of the South, as hopeless, inferior, pitiable.

Strengths
- Aid is crucial in short-term emergencies, such as famines or floods.
- Aid can help overcoming infrastructure problems. Developing economies need a good transport system, but may be too poor to build one themselves. They get stuck in a vicious circle of low investments and low production. Aid can help leapfrog this problem
- Aid is a useful, though limited, form of redistribution in an incredibly unequal world
- Aid is an expression of empathy between North and South.

Increasingly, participants agree that government aid should be matched and combined with private sector money, invested by companies. This would draw on skills of the private sector in managing investment projects, while public sector money would steer them to socially beneficial projects.

Current debates

Over the last ten years, a new consensus has been developing in North and South about the future of international aid. Here are some of the main ideas:

- **Aid should be tied to good governance.** Northern governments and international organisations are trying to link aid with the human rights record of recipient states

- **Aid should be directed towards alleviating poverty.** Aid programmes should be designed to alleviate poverty. Small local rural programmes of education and development are preferred to huge industrial projects, such as building dams.

- **Aid should be directed towards the interests of women.** Improving women's education and health is a very effective ways of controlling population growth

- **Development from below.** Where possible, aid programmes should be directed to local, voluntary, self-help organisations rather than via central government agencies.

Practice questions

1 If there were no political parties we would need to invent them. Discuss. (4 marks)

2 'Prison works' The Rt. Hon Michael Howard, Secretary of State for Home Affairs, 1993-1997. Do you agree? (2–4 marks)

3 Examine the case for and against the UK joining the Single European Currency. (4-6 marks)

4 Why has the world economy become more globalised in the last fifty years? (4–6 marks)

5 International Aid causes more problems than it solves. Discuss. (4 marks)

6 What caused the International Debt Crisis? (6 marks)

7 Reforms of the National Health Service have consistently failed to address the systems structural problems. Discuss. (6 marks)

8 Do we live in a society that finds it impossible to make coherent moral judgements? If so why. If not, why not? (6 marks)

9 'Laws are made to be broken'. Under what circumstances, if any, is it justifiable to break the law? (10 marks)

10 Poor countries are poor because their governments are corrupt. To what extent is this a plausible argument? (10 marks)

11 What explains the emergence of the UK welfare state? (4–6 marks)

12 'If it ain't broke don't fix it.' Is this an appropriate response to the UK's unwritten constitution? (6 marks)

Answers to practice questions

Culture morality, arts & humanities

1   It is very tempting to answer a question like this using your own personal opinions' but beware! Although you are welcome to state what you think, make sure that your viewpoint is objective, not a personal rant and that your answer shows an understanding of the pop industry. For example:

- Begin with a brief introductory paragraph which directly addresses the question,
  'It would be unfair to say that all pop groups today are devoid of artistic talent, but there is certainly a strong case to argue that many new groups owe their success more to hype and technology than artistic talent.'
- Explain the popular music phenomenon: how and why it began, relating this to the key idea in the question - was popular music created as a vehicle to channel artistic talent or take advantage of a new niche market?
- Discuss why popular music is popular - for example, because of the way it is packaged; because of its lyrics etc.
- Describe what else you think mass success depends upon e.g. Djs, play lists, journalists etc.
- Develop your argument by using examples of groups that are currently popular - in your opinion (remember to be objective) do they have artistic talent or have they been manufactured to appeal to a certain audience?
- Examine the alternatives to manufactured pop - in your opinion are there any pop groups who do have artistic talent and why?
- Conclude by readdressing the question and saving your personal viewpoint - the deciding factor of the argument - until the end. Make sure what you say is convincing.

2   To answer this question you need to have a good sense of what you believe and which moral code you live by yourself. You can attack this question in a number of ways for example:

- use your knowledge of moral philosophy to structure your thoughts and ideas about whether C21st needs morals;
- look at the newspapers at the issues that involve some sort of moral decision - then decide what would happen if we lived in a world without them.

Structure is as important as content in a General Studies essay because examiners are as interested in your ability to present a coherent argument as they are about what you have to say. Remember your skills at thinking and powers of analysis should be emphasised. One way of impressing an examiner is by writing in perfect paragraphs. A perfect paragraph should contain:

- a topic sentence - which makes clear the point that the paragraph is going to discuss;
- supporting sentences which expand upon the subject of the topic sentence;
- a final sentence that suggests what will be addressed in the next paragraph.For example,

'Many choices that you make are a straightforward matter of personal preference and the resulting actions are neither moral or immoral. They only become moral choices when you consider the intentions behind them, the results they will bring and the values of society or the individuals they reflect. Therefore, when you are not sure as to the consequences of your actions, you may then be faced with a moral dilemma and have to discriminate between good and bad to be able to give reasons for your actions. It is these moral judgments that affect the way we think about certain issues and act in certain ways.'

3   Always be objective with such emotive arguments, showing both sides.

Remember, the examiner is not expecting a pathway to religious harmony or world peace, just evidence to show that you have understood the question and the issues involved.

Plan your essay carefully so that you:

- don't waste time on irrelevant points;
- make sure you've covered the issues evenly;
- have a clear idea about what you need to say.

Organise your notes under subheadings.

Choose points that you can expand upon and provide exemplification:

Good points:

- Religion supports the unwritten rules about how you should live your life, e.g. on adultery, murder or theft – all statutory laws;
- Religion gives meaning to life - especially to the bereaved;
- Religious congregations provide a meeting place, create a feeling of community and comfort the lonely – essential when the idea of 'community' is being eroded.

Bad points:

- Religion causes violence, warfare and death – e.g. Northern Ireland and the Middle East;
- Wars show that religion can cause bigotry and intolerance in people on a large scale and an individual level – e.g. Croatia;
- Karl Marx saw religion as 'the opium of the people' – showing an historical perspective.

Evaluate your evidence. Your conclusion will depend very much on how you view religion or if you consider yourself religious. If you are still unsure, you may find it easier to evaluate the arguments on a global and at an individual level.

4   For good marks you will need to show the examiner what you know about the advertising industry as well as being able to express your own point of view. Try to give examples from adverts that you know to back up your arguments. Points that you could include are:

- a definition of advertising which states the main objective of advertising: to reach a wide audience and to make money;
- an account of the effect that advertising has on society and how it could reinforce dominant ideology - not giving the audience much credit;
- the use of stereotypical images in adverts which can cause offense by creating dissatisfaction with life amongst the more vulnerable sections of society;
- a discussion about the powerful imagery that conveys cultural values e.g. about gender roles and how this can be offensive to both genders;
- how market research is used to create lifestyle images that will appeal to target audiences and encourage them to buy into the promise of this lifestyle by purchasing the product or service - making people who do not aspire to 'advert world' seem socially inadequate.

TIP - Remember to use quotations where you can. You could begin your conclusion with a Rita Clifton quotation and base your summarising argument around it e.g. that advertisers are only feeding back to us images of ourselves - so do we blame advertising companies for causing offense or do we blame society? Make up your own mind.

5   To answer this question you need to be able to show quite a specialist knowledge of the media about:

- television news programmes
- news values
- viewing figures and audiences

A rounded answer could consider:

- the nature, popularity and importance of news programmes;
- the importance of viewing figures for a programme's survival, as reflected by the recent ratings war

between the BBC and ITV;
- the popular saying 'No news is good news';
- how news items are chosen and news programmes structured around them;
- examples of the range of stories in recent news bulletins that you have watched.
- how 'news values' are related to what audiences want and therefore viewing figures;
- how far you agree with the question; a conclusion could be as follows:'It is therefore clear that television news is largely dictated by negative 'news values' unless the most immediate and topical story of the day is positive, for example, if England won the World Cup. We cannot escape the fact that the news is a media product, created to attract as many viewers as possible and to make a profit. It is therefore as manipulative as any other media product and delivers what it believes its audience wants. Perhaps therefore, its focus on negative issues is more of an indictment on society than on the programmes that bring us the news.'

6   This question is asking for an understanding of what the modern art movement is about. You should use specialist knowledge and strengthen your account by using examples of modern art that you know. Answers could include:

- a definition of modern art and how it differs from more traditional 'fine art';
- how and why modern art began and who were/are its most influential characters (e.g. Picasso, Warhol, Hirst etc);
- the subjects of modern art, for example, the preference for installations over paintings and the emphasis on everyday items;
- the function to shock and the media hype surrounding it;
- other contributory factors that further help to explain the growing popularity of modern art for example, its attempt to express the issues of our time in a new, realistic way befitting the C21st;
- and you could conclude that:
- its ultimate function is as a popular art form that anyone can understand, even if they don't like it;
- it has a function to make you think and so has value even if you are thinking about whether it is really art or something less impressive;
- or if you have an alternative point of view....use it! You may well have other valid points of your own, which examiners will give you credit for, even if they don't appear on the exam board's actual mark scheme. Remember – more mark will be added as you demonstrate your ability to think and analyse.

7 You can clearly tap into your own experience of school and option choices at GCSE – I am sure there have been times when you wished that you had opted for a different subject for some reason and it is this ideas that you will need. Coupled to this information, you should have a clear idea of how studying art and music could enrich your education/life:

- you could begin with some ideas about the value of aesthetic enjoyment;
- how studying a breadth of subjects will create a more rounded person;
- how they are culturally enriching activities that students may continue doing for themselves;
- how appreciation of these subjects could avoid ignorance and prejudice to grow in relation to the arts;
- or even how retaining a breadth of study until the end of compulsory schooling could maximise marketability on the job market or increase degree subject choice.It is as important as ever not to launch into a personal diatribe: keep your view objective and make sure what you say is clear and understandable to all.

TIP: when you are arguing make sure you only say one thing at a time: keep one idea to one sentence; avoid long rambling sentences; avoid sounding pompous but also do not use slang; accentuate the positive not the negative - this will keep your writing lively and interesting to read - your examiner will appreciate this!

8 This question gives you the option of choosing to write about the type of art you know most about, so you should be able to capitalise on this. What you need to remember is that your reasons for liking the work of art must be convincing. The best way to sound convincing is:

- to have a sound understanding of the critical framework needed to appreciate your chosen work of art
- to show that you actually did enjoy it.
- You must therefore convince the examiner of the value of a piece of work and why it appealed to you.

If your writing simply describes the work of art, retells the story of the play, or relates the key changes in a piece of music then you are not likely to gain high marks. A good answer therefore needs to analyse and comment on the reason your work of art is worthy of that title. You should use knowledge from other AS level subjects within this domain to help you formulate your answer and it is expected that if you choose this question, that you will bring a certain level of appropriate, specialist vocabulary to your writing.

You could structure your essay:

- INTRODUCTION: what is the work of art and by what criteria will you judge it;
- MAIN BODY: describe, comment on and analyse the work of art with an indication of your aesthetic and emotional response to it;
- CONCLUSION: use your best point and summarise just what it is about this work of art that you find so enjoyable.

Maths

1 Angle representing everything = 230°

Amount represented by $1° = \frac{3\,600\,000}{230} = £15,652$

Cost of advertising = £2034,783

2 $0.3 \times 0.6 = 0.18$

3 Horizontal reading:

Lane 1:	Van 3m	Coach 12m	Car 3m
Lane 2:	Car 3m	Truck 8m	Car 4m	Car 3m
Lane 3:	Lorry 12m	Van 4m	Car 3m

Vehicles left: Coach 10m and Car 3m

In order of size:

Lane 1:	Coach 12m	Truck 8m	
Lane 2:	Lorry 12m	Car 4m	Van 4m
Lane 3:	Coach 10m	Van 3m	Car 3m	Car 3m

One less vehicle is loaded.

4 80% = £345

$20\% = £\frac{345}{4} = £86.25$

original cost = £86.25 × 5 = £431.25

5 1 ton = 2240 pounds = 2240 × 454 g = 1016960 g = 1016.96 kg

difference = 16.96 kg

6 Distance = 128km

Bearing = 129°

7 Sample is too small.

Reading the paper does not imply that you have bought the paper.

How can you be sure you have a representative sample of the population?

8 Sum of first 50 integers = $\frac{50}{2} \times 51 = 1275$

The value of 20 + 21 + 22 + 23 + ...+ 49 + 50:
$1275 - \frac{19}{12} \times 20 = 1085$

9

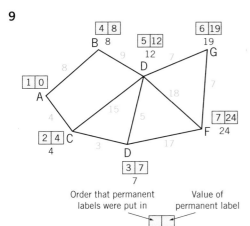

Order that permanent labels were put in   Value of permanent label

Algorithm

Step 1 Label the start node A with zero. Indicate permanent label with a box.

Step 2 Put a temporary label on all nodes that can be reached directed from the node just given a permanent label.

        Temporary label = permanent label + arc length to neighbouring node.

Step 3 Select node with smallest temporary label and make that permanent.

Step 4 Repeat steps 2 and 3 until all nodes have permanent labels.

Shortest distance A to F = 24 Route ACEF

Science

1 (a)

2 It filters out harmful ultra-violet radiation from the suns rays.

3 Charles Darwin

4 This question requires you to briefly state two arguments. Expand on any two of the following points:
- GE crops are thoroughly tested – so we know they are safe
- GE crops will allow us to increase what we produce from agriculture, which means we will be able to feed the rapidly growing world population
- crops which are resistant to disease or pests can be developed, allowing us to be sure that the crops we plant will grow properly
- GE crops will require less chemicals so are better for the environment
- GE crops may allow us to develop medical applications

5 Expand a little on any two of the following points:
- nuclear power is unsafe – the example of Chernobyl proves this
- nuclear power is unnecessary – if we developed alternatives and reduced our use of energy in total we would not need to use nuclear power
- nuclear power is polluting – radioactivity has been released into the atmosphere and sea in Britain (you could find out about an example to support this – try Sellafield as a starting point)
- nuclear waste has to be stored for thousands of years – how can we be certain that it will be secure when we don't have the technology to be able to store it yet
- global warming means our nuclear power stations are at risk from flooding as they are mainly on the coast

6 You're looking for a slightly longer answer here, perhaps with some more developed examples. This could be the focus for an essay style question.
- You need to explain how scientists build up knowledge over time by using direct observation to formulate hypotheses and then attempt to validate them (scientific method and inductive method). Make sure you use technical terms – don't be vague.
- Other scientists can test these methods and advance the theories and ideas.
- The build up of knowledge is a slow process with

deliberate steps being made – e.g. progress in the Human Genome Project
- Scientific laws are developed to guide further research
- Mention Kuhn and Popper and how paradigms are developed and the concept that scientific knowledge can only be disproved, never completely proven

7 Use more developed examples. You need to be clear that you understand what inductive methods are – perhaps begin with a brief statement explaining how they work and providing an example (e.g. Galileo or Darwin). Key points are:
- ingenuity and scientific brilliance are held back by the need to observe everything directly
- if you have no way of testing something you can't propose it – this may hold back the development of understanding or further research
- scientists may work in isolation rather than in co-operation

8a 0.6°C (remember to include the units!). This graph isn't actually showing temperatures but the rise in temperature. Make sure you read the axis carefully.

8b You need to be much more specific:
- the overall trend is upward but with fluctuation (it's going up and down)
- between 1901 and 1925 there was a general upward trend from about half a degree below normal to about normal
- from 1925 to about 1975 the line is around normal, fluctuating either side on a year by year basis
- from 1975 the trend is for a fairly sharp rise to a maximum of 0.6 degrees above normal
Remember to read the question – you're not being asked why this is happening.

8c There are only 4 marks available so you need to be efficient in your answer.
- greenhouse gases in the atmosphere trap heat – the natural greenhouse effect
- greenhouse gases include Carbon Dioxide
- human activity – including the burning of fossil fuels – is increasing the concentration of greenhouse gases in the atmosphere
- which may be leading to a increase in global temperature – there are more greenhouse gases so more heat is trapped. This is global warming.

8d Use the following points to expand on:
- global temperatures have fluctuated in the past – fossil records and tree rings
- this could simply be a natural fluctuation
- we only have accurate records from about 1850
- we don't know how the global system will respond – natural feedback systems such as plankton may kick in
- the global atmospheric system is complex and we don't fully understand it.

9 Define genetically modified (or engineered) means (the modification of the internal structure of plants by direct human interference in order to develop a 'better' strain of plant – for example, one resistant to frost). Then concentrate on the following points:
- food may not be labelled – some supermarkets are doing so, other may not;
- some supermarkets are banning all GE food
- develop the role of government in food labelling and safety – are their any governmental restrictions on the use of GE ingredients or the use of crops grown in GE trials in food products?
- problems exist because some products (e.g. imported soya from the USA) are not distinguished between GE soya and 'natural' soya
- some products are present in such small quantities that it's difficult to tell if they are modified or not
- there may be contamination of natural crops by GE crops, leading to effective GE crops being present even in 'organic' plants
- how long is the food chain – do you consider a cow "natural" even if it has eaten GE produce in it's diet? Would meat from that cow be labelled as GE?

10 This is a question that deals with the idea of improving technology in the communications and media sphere. Discuss the following points, briefly:
- e-mail – quick, efficient and informal but requires technology and their are confidentiality issues
- letter – generally fairly quick by fist class, cheap but time consuming to write
- telephone – personal but potentially expensive
- fax – formal but quick and can be used for visual images – requires technology
- ultimately there may be the possibility of video links etc being developed

11 You need to balance your argument between scientific opinion that evolution is probably correct and the idea that there are opposing points of view. You can also explain how scientific ideas work and that science, according to Popper for example, must be capable of being disproven. The idea that evolution is a paradigm and that we may be able to advance that paradigm at some point in the future could also be developed.

12 This question requires you to think about some of the ways in which science could be misused, to begin with. There are lots of examples, but you could include:

- nuclear weapons – or the development of military technology in general
- human cloning and it's potential implication
- genetic engineering of food and it's implications for ecosystems
- technology like that of the gas chamber

There are examples of science which are deemed 'good' but which can have unfortunate repercussions:

- burning of fossil fuels
- over use of anti-biotics

The important thing in a question like this is to provide examples from both sides of the argument and then sum up how far you agree. Think about whether scientists have a responsibility to limit their work if they fear that it may be misused at any point in the future or whether they should attempt to explore science no matter what the potential uses are.

Human cloning is a good example – are the medical benefits worth the ethical problems which may come about if complete humans were ever cloned?

The development of nuclear power came about as a result of the research into atomic weapons at the end of the second world war. Many of the scientists who worked on this project felt reticent about the work.

What about scientists who worked on research in Nazi concentration camps? Although we might appal their methods they advanced scientific ideas successfully.

13 Make sure you develop enough examples in your answer to back up the points you're making. There's no point simply making a few arguments for a longer question – this is where examples come into their own. Think about points like:

- we have no real alternative at present
- fossil fuels are convenient and easy to use
- there are large supplies of fossil fuels and we seem to keep on finding more
- we have plenty of time to develop alternatives – as scientific knowledge moves on we'll be more able to use these (e.g. electric cars)
- we don't yet have alternatives in some areas – such as for petrol
- there is tenuous evidence that fossil fuels cause global environmental problems
- fossil fuels are cheap – we need cheap energy to allow our economics to boom
- we can produce lots of power from fossil fuels
- nuclear power is the major alternative – which is dangerous and expensive.

On the other hand:

- fossil fuels are finite and will run out
- how can we put our own needs in front of those of future generations?
- there is increasing evidence that global climate change is going to cause significant problems for future generations
- fossil fuels are dirty and pollute our local environments
- we can use less fossil fuels – energy efficiency, using public transport, banning cars from city centres etc.
- the over use of fossil fuels benefits big corporations who produce them most – they make money today and harm tomorrows economy which will not be able to use cheap fossil fuels
- not enough money has been put into research for alternatives to fossil fuels – we should spend more here
- fossil fuels are mainly used by MEDCs who would like to restrict their use by LEDCs. Is this about the environment or is it more to do with keeping LEDCs in their place as cheap labour sources for our big corporations?

15 There are a wide range of examples you could use to support your answer:

- human genetics
- GE food
- nuclear power
- IVF
- the application of technology to solve problems associated with hazards such as hurricanes or problems such as the reliable supply of clean water.

To criticise the statement you could consider:

- issues associated with environmental pollution – cars are an advantage but are the pollution issues worth the cost to society
- technology can isolate individuals – e.g. internet technology is all very well but does it mean we sit at computers rather than interacting with people
- technology is dependent upon access – does everyone have access to technology or is it just the rich and powerful who have access – thus retaining their position on power as a result?

Politics and economics

1   Think first, what does the statement really mean. In this case the examiners are asking you to do a bit of decoding first and want you to reframe the statement as a clear set of intellectual problems

One way of thinking about this is: Political parties form a vitally important element of a successful political system. We may not like them very much, and there may be problems with them, but if we lived in an imaginary political world in which there were no political parties we would have to invent something that looked pretty similar to today's political parties if we wanted to function successfully.

SO who can you think about that. The first thing to do is to think about is what are political parties. But what is that political parties actually do. We know that they compete for power, but they have other functions and purposes that help politics be a manageable meaningful process.

Spend some time listing the key features of political parties and their key functions. Where you can make sure you have some empirical examples of political parties performing those functions.

Think about what political and social life would be like without political parties. What problems would we encounter? Can you imagine other kinds of organisation replacing political parties and all the things they do – like pressure groups for example? What problems might they encounter? What limits might there be to their political usefulness.

Make sure you conclude by returning to the question in its own terms. You don't have to agree. You might want to say that if we were to invent political parties again we might make them look very different from today's parties. That's a good strong point to make but then make sure you explain what those differences would be and why they would constitute an improvement on today's political parties.

2   First you need to decode the question a bit. What exactly did Michael Howard mean? You need to flesh out his point of view, i.e. that Prison is an effective deterrent to crime and probably that Prison is an appropriate punishment and a plausible way of reforming criminals.

However you decode the question make sure that you structure your response to the question around this.

Think about the kinds of evidence you could draw upon that would either support Howard's argument or provide an argument against.

Is there evidence, for example, that by increasing the rate of imprisonment or the length of sentences leads to a lower crime rate?

Note you can make your argument more sophisticated (which examiners will like) if you think about different kinds of prison and prison experience. It might be that some kinds of prison work and some don't. Similarly, it may be that for some people prison works and for some it doesn't. Ask yourself what types of prison and what evidence you can draw upon.

Finally, note the question asks, "Do you agree?" so make sure that you conclude your essay by responding precisely to that question.

3   As this is a short question you need to very precise when answering.

The question asks you to examine the case for and against, so make sure that you do both of these things and that you allocate them roughly equal space.

Note, the question doesn't ask you to explain what exactly the single currency is, so assume that your reader already knows that background information get straight down to examining the pros and cons of the argument.

Decide before you start how you are going to structure your answer. You could give all the reasons for and then all the reasons against. Or you could mix them up going through the debate issue by issue and then stating the different positions on each point.

Note, a really good answer to this question would note that different groups within the UK will benefit or suffer differently under the single European currency so note areas of variation: i.e. what is good for some businesses might not be good for others, or there might be differences between one group of workers and another.

4   This is a short answer so get straight down the question.

You should try and define, briefly and concisely what exactly you mean by globalisation. If your not sure make sure you go back to your notes and work out a short sharp definition from which you can begin

Note this is not a discuss or evaluate question you don't have to waste words coming to an opinion about whether globalisation is a good thing or not, or who it effects.

Make sure you focus on the core of the question which is explanatory. Examiners will be looking for an explanation of why the world economy is globalised.

Before you start writing brainstorm – think through all the possible arguments that could explain globalisation.

Make sure as you write up your answer that you really re delivering an explanation – that there is a chain of reasoning that leads the reader from a cause to an outcome. Its not enough just to say that transport has changed in the last fifty years. You need to say what transport has changed, how does that practically impact on what businesses, markets and individuals do.

5   First note that this is not a simple international aid is a good thing or a bad thing type of question, its asking you do something a bit more than that. The question already acknowledges that international aid can solve some problems but might also create problems.

The key thing in a question like this is a to come to a balanced judgement by the end of it- does it create more problems than it solves, does it create less problems than it solves. It doesn't' matter which side of the argument you come down on as long as you come down on one side of the argument through a plausible chain of reasoning.

When you are preparing the answer make sure you draw up a list of problems caused by aid and problems it might solve.

However, don't think that you can answer the question by just listing these things or saying that there is more on one s list than another. You need to take things a stage further by thinking about the magnitude of the problems solved or created. If something causes one huge problem but solves many small problems it's likely that the causing problems list is actually more significant than the solving problems list.

Make sure you have a conclusion at the end of your essay, drawing these strands together.

6   This is a simply stated question. It just wants you to explain why something happened.

Start by defining what we actually mean by the international debt crisis. Make sure you have some key dates, places, figures etc. To explain exactly what it is you want to explain.

A basic answer to this question will be a narrative, a story that leads us from one set of event s to another.

Whatever else you answer has it should have a basic chronology of what happened, where.

To push your grade up and impress the examiner you will want to invest that narrative with some clear explanations of how one set of events translate into another – what we call causation.

In something as complex as the international debt crisis there are likely to be multiple causes and multiple events interacting with each other. Better essays on this kind of question will make an explicit judgement about which causes were the most important. Even better, where there were opportunities for things to be different, where key actors made key decisions try and identify them. Or try and differentiate between short term and long-term causes.

7   What does the question really mean? Again, you need to decode examiner's language into normal English.

The key term is "structural problems". What are they? The examiners want you to think about long-term, persistent problems in the NHS. These might include problems created by the original administrative structure of the NHS, like the enormous power of doctors rather than managers.

Or it might refer to the built in bias of the system towards curative rather than preventive medicine.

Or, it might refer to the demographic problem that the NHS consistently faces – that the population is getting older and older and therefore, in health terms more and more expensive.

Before you start decide which structural problems you are going to focus on. You should probably cover at least two or three but not more than four.

Then you need to think about demonstrating whether the reforms of the NHS have addressed these problems or not. This bit of the question is open. You might want to argue that the internal market reforms of the 1990s have addressed the doctor/manager problem. Or you might want to argue that it is unreasonable to expect the NHS to deal with preventative medicine, which is really the responsibility of individuals.

Whichever way you go remember to keep focused on the question and not get distracted with a lot of information that is not relevant.

8   There are a lot of clauses in this question. So before you start take your time to go through the question so that your essay plan reflects the concerns of the question.

The core is the idea that our society can't make coherent moral judgements. What does that mean? It is not asking you to look at individuals but at our collective moral life, The big moral debates that engage the media, social groups of all kinds, politicians etc.

Then ask yourself what does it mean by coherent. The question is suggesting that our society cannot come to a consensus on big moral questions (like abortion or the rights and wrongs of genetic technologies or the rights and wrongs of the death penalty). That there are significant and perhaps unbridgeable differences.

Then you need to decide whether this is the case or not. If it is the case then you need to follow that argument through. If you disagree with the statement you need to argue that through. Either way you need to decide what case you are going to make and construct your argument.

The case against might be that actually for a very large complex diverse society we do actually agree on a lot of things a lot of the time, but that this makes for poor news and debate and therefore we tend to underestimate the areas we agree on and overemphasis those areas we disagree about.

The case for might lead you to argue that we have become a much more diverse society in lots of ways with many different moral systems and values – the decline of Christianity and the rise of fringe religions might point to this. Or you might want to argue that mainstream political ideologies have declined in their capacity to respond to new moral problems.

Taking this on a stage – for extra marks – you might want to argue that the world has just become more complex. That our grandparent's generation never had to deal with new technologies, globalisation etc…

9 At last a relatively straightforward question. The quote is just a stimulus to thought. The real business is in the statement after the quote.

You might want to begin by stating briefly what we mean by the law and what we mean by crime as a way of opening the question up. Where crime is defined in normative terms rather than legal terms it is possible to imagine a conflict between the letter of the law and a system of moral values.

You should definitely gather together some key empirical examples of cases where the law has been broken and the participants felt it was justified. Civil disobedience by suffragettes, peace protesters or civil rights activists might be an example.

You could also look at individual cases. Women who have chosen to have an abortion in societies that make it illegal. Individuals who have drunk alcohol in societies that have outlawed its production and consumption etc.

Then you need to draw out from your examples some systematic arguments about why people think law

breaking might be justified. Because the ways in which the rules have been made are illegitimate. Because the laws perpetrate a greater moral evil. Because the law infringes what are perceived to be individual rights and liberties.

But don't forget all the counter arguments: that we tamper with the rule of law at our peril for example.

10 The key thing to think about in this in of question is the bit that says "to what extent is this a plausible argument" The examiners want you to examine the initial statement but then they want you to take it a stage further and say, not is it right or wrong, but how right or how wrong

It could be that the argument is simply correct or simply wrong or that it is only partially right and that a lot of other arguments need to be drawn upon to explain poverty. Even then you will need to decide whether government corruption is a very important, important or slightly important factor.

You can begin by thinking about corrupt governments first. Are all poor countries cursed with corrupt government? What about rich countries that have corrupt governments (there are plenty of those). And in any case you need to think through why corruption should lead to poverty. The chain of reasoning needs to be explicit.

Then you should think about why there is corruption, what does it actually mean. Are there systematic reasons for corruption, causes that go back into history?

And then you think about other causes of poverty that may not be related at all. Above all you need to bring all of these arguments together into a balanced conclusion that actually makes a judgement about the relative importance of corruption as against other factors and explanations.

11 This is a short question so get down to business right away. Sort out a definition of what we mean by the welfare state and its key features in the UK, i.e.; the public sector provision of health, education, housing, social security etc.

The set a time frame, what are you going to explain. You might want to say that the UK welfare state has emerged in a series of jumps – the liberal government reforms, the post 45 reforms etc. Each of these will need a separate explanation.

Then you need to think about causes. Always a good idea to divide these into short term and long term. In the case of the liberal reforms long-term causes are the impact of a capitalist industrial revolution on life in the city and the collapse of old systems of welfare. Short-term causes would be the shock of the poor quality of recruits to the British Army.

You might also want to note the importance of wars, active political campaigning, key individuals, the impact of new ideas.

For top marks you might want to briefly note that different societies produce different welfare states and that the UK welfare state took a particular form because key social groups managed to win the day over other groups (contrast the US, German, Swedish experience with the UK)

12 Once again decode the question. The argument being made is that the UK constitution basically works and if something as complex and delicate as a constitution basically works it is better to keep warts and all, rather than to try a create something completely new with all the dangers and uncertainties that large scale, social reform brings with it.

So in deciding whether this appropriate response you need to decide. Is the UK constitution broken, faulty, problematic? Even if it is, is it clear that the possible alternatives will be at least no worse than the current situation? To put it another way, will constitutional reform create more problems than it solves?

Now think about reasons why the constitution might be a problem. There are lots: the problems of first part the post vs. proportional representation. The undefined place of the monarchy. The need for more systematic written forms of our rights and responsibilities. The problem of the House of Lords – do we need one, should it be elected etc.

Now think about reasons why embarking on constitutional reform might be a problem. The system has worked pretty well so far. We have alternating governments. We have never had a dictatorship, but plenty of societies with written constitution have had dictatorships - Weimar Germany and the Soviet Union for example. The unwritten constitution provides flexibility. It provides a place for custom and tradition. There are very big disagreements about what a new constitution might look like so some people are bound to be very unhappy with change is that good for political stability etc.

Remember. You need to sum up the arguments on both sides in a conclusion. Try and take a look at web sites, newspaper articles etc, on the issue and try and make your argument as up to date as possible.

Glossary

numerator the upper part of a fraction.

objective views, not distorted by personal bias.

observation scientific process of watching events.

ostracise the removal of somebody from society by other people, either physically or socially.

ozone layer layer of gases in the upper atmosphere that filters UV rays.

paradigm a set of ideas that are generally believed at one time.

passive consumers people who watch a any media experience without involving themselves in it.

persecution harassment of people due to a difference of belief or ideas.

playlists lists of the singles that will get airplay, produced every week by radio stations.

polynomial an algebraic expression consisting of a number of terms.

popular culture the opposite of high culture, also known as low culture, being the works of writers, artists and composers who are considered to appeal to a mass audience from all areas of society.

power (or exponent or index) the number of reduced size which indicates how many times a number has to be multiplied by itself.

prejudices reconceived ideas, as a bias to something, without action.

Programme music depicts specific objects and events.

Protestant a member of any of the faiths based on the Christian religions.

Quaker a member of the society of friends.

random genetic mutation describes the alteration of the genetic code by chance.

Referentialists believe that music produces statements.

representation an artist interprets an aspect of reality, either accurately or abstractly.

rhythm the beat, which gives music pace and timing.

Romantic music from this period was cerebral, unrestrained and even melodramatic.

satire entertainment in which topical issues, folly or evil are held up to scorn by means of ridicule and irony.

scalene triangle no two sides or angles of this triangle are the same.

secular in reference against religion.

significant figure the accuracy of a number.

Single European Act aimed to remove trade barriers and create a single European market by 1992.

Situationism suggests that the only thing that makes an act right or wrong is the presence or absence of love.

social control religion supports written laws, by forbidding crimes such as murder and theft.

stomata the hole created by two guard cells on a leaf, used for gas exchange between the plant and the atmosphere.

strike force people who promote single and album sales to retail outlets.

subjective having views that are influenced by
substitution the process of replacing the letters in an equation by other values.

sustainable development the development of people's lives, while respecting the environment.

Symbolism art that uses symbolic images.

target group groups of particular class, age, occupation and gender-related groups whose habits can be recognised.

The round a theatre with a central stage, surrounded by the audience.

The Treaty of Rome signed by the original 6 countries of the EU to focus on the creation of a common market and economic integration.

tone the quality, pitch and volume.

tragedy a play in which the protagonist falls to disaster due to personal failing and circumstances; any drama dealing with serious or sombre themes and ending with disaster.

traits a characteristic feature or quality of a person or thing.

Uses and gratifications model when you watch a film you do so to fulfil your own needs.

Utilitarianism the doctrine that morality is all about securing the maximum happiness for the maximum number of people.

validation the approval of something based on a test.

values refers to issues that are not just about individuals' preferences, but collective ideas about what constitutes a 'good' society and a 'good' life

variables the factors that are altered during an experiment.

vox pops a techniques to get a quotes that represent popular opinions.

World Trade Organisation an organisation which seeks to promote free trade between nations and monitors world trade.

responsible for finding, developing and looking after bands, as well as managing image, sound, press outings and publicity.

Absolute music depicts moods and a general meaning rather than specific events.

acid rain sulphur dioxide and various nitrogen oxides dissolve in rain, making it acidic.

aesthetics the philosophical study of beauty and taste in all branches of 'the arts'.

afterlife the idea that the soul carries on living after the death of the body

algebraic expression an equation using numbers and letters.

analysis the process of testing data.

bar chart graphs using bars to show value.

Baroque dignified and courtly music.

base single units that create the genetic code.

bigotry intolerance of another being.

binomial algebraic expression with two factors.

Buddhism religious teaching spread by the Buddha; man can achieve perfect enlightenment by destroying greed, hatred and delusion, since these are the causes of all suffering.

capital crimes offence that carries the death penalty.

Catholics a member of the Latin Church.

Christianity religion based on one God.

chromosomes the structure of DNA in animals.

Classical music with balanced and restrained sounds and any highly acclaimed art form.

cloning the isolation of a gene or set of genes and the implantation into another organism.

comedy work of light and amusing character; a play whose main characters triumph over adversity.

common culture any set of inherited or derived beliefs, values, ideas and knowledge that are shared by certain groups within society.

conceptual understanding a set of rules for evaluating and understanding objects.

conclusion a decision, based on an experiment.

conditional probability the occurrence of two events are dependent on each other.

conservative a tendency to be moderate and to live by long-held value systems.

context when something has a particular relevance or meaning in a certain situation.

continuous data that can take any value and range.

convention a form of proceeding based on the past occurrences of a similar item.

creationism the belief that the universe was created by a god.

creative insight the jump to a conclusion without the direct observation.

custodial sentence a sentence, served in an institution.

democratic a state run by a group of people, voted into place by the people.

denominator the lower part of a fraction .

Deregulation removing regulations or restrictions.

discrete data that can take only certain values.

Divine command theory a belief that killing, stealing, causing injury and so on are immoral because such acts are forbidden in religious writings and are against your God's will.

DNA deoxyribosenucleic acid is the macromolecule that holds the genetic code.

drama a sequence of events that is emotional, tragic or turbulent.

dramatic irony used in comedy, the audience is privy to information that the characters are not.

emmisions release of gases into the atmosphere.

Emotivism the idea that moral judgements are not made universally. Expressing a personal feeling that has been triggered by emotion.

EMU European Monetary Union a collaboration between European countries.

equilateral triangle a triangle with all three sides equal and all three angles of equal size.

ethics logical defence of feelings on the basis of right or wrong.

evolution the term used to describe the change in characteristics of an organism over time.

Existentialism no universal rules and individuals choose a course of action and in doing so exhibit what they believe to be their own morals.

expression showing a feeling, belief or symbol.

genes the single units that create a protein.

genome entire set of chromosomes in an organism.

genre a style of art or literature.

globalisation the process of enabling businesses, and financial and investment markets to operate internationally.

gradient the steepness of a graph.

greenhouse effect heating up of the atmosphere.

Group of Seven (G7) or G8 countries 7 leading industrial countries, Canada, France, Germany, Italy, Japan, US and UK (and Russia if G8).

harmony supports the tune and produces complementary sounds.

high culture the works of writers, artists and composers who are considered by scholars and critics to be superior to others.

Hinduism predominantly Indian religion based on the worship of many Gods, belief in reincarnation and a caste system.

hypercompetition the disruption of existing markets by flexible, fast-moving businesses.

hypodermic model suggests that meanings are 'injected' in to your minds.

hypothesis speculative theory based on observation.

ideologies ideas that form the basis of theories.

imagery the use of symbols to create a concept.

impartiality treating both sides of an argument equally.

imperial the old English form of measurement.

improper fraction a fraction with a larger numerator than denominator.

independent events there is no relevance on an event happening, by another event.

individual identity the association of something to give a meaning to life.

induction argument based on direct observation.

Intuitionalism actions are right if they are useful or for the benefit of the majority.

Islam the religion of Muslims, having the Koran as its sacred scripture.

isosceles triangle two sides of this triangle are equal and two of the angles are equal, with one line of symmetry.

Judaism the religion of the Jews, based on the Old Testament of the Bible.

Kantianism moral action defines itself and is something that is good in its own right.

Karl Marx 19th Century thinker and revolutionary.

Maastricht Treaty document signed to promote closer economic and political co-operation between the Member Countries.

mainstream film feature-length narrative created for entertainment and profit and is generally associated with Hollywood.

map locating genes in reference to the genome.

market trading or selling opportunities provided by a particular group of people.

mass the majority of people.

mean an average formed by the sum of all the data divided by the number of items of data.

median an average formed from data ordered from the smallest to the largest. The median is the item of data in the middle.

Medieval, Mystery and Morality plays religious stories, preaching that virtue overcomes greed.

melody tune or distinctive arrangement of notes.

Member States member countries of the EU.

metric measurement based on multiples of ten.

minority group that is significantly smaller than and has different viewpoints to those of the mass.

mixed number a number which uses whole numbers and fractions.

mode the average formed as the item which occurs most often in a set of data.

monoculture farming, dependent on one crop.

mood emotions or feelings that art can evoke.

moral human behaviour that distinguishes between right and wrong behaviour.

moral philosophy the conduct of humans, depending on the logical decision of an action, based on right and wrong.

morality knowledge and practice of what is moral, according to your personal view.

multinational businesses large companies that operate in several countries.

national culture traits peculiar to a nation.

nationalism common cultural characteristics that bind a population together.

Natural law it's human nature to live by moral principles.

natural selection evolution, by which a trait, which creates an advantage for an organism, causes it to reproduce successfully.

neutrality both sides of the argument are presented equally, in an impartial and way.

news values the priority placed on a news story, depending on its impact, quality and content.

non-referentialism music exists alone and has no extra-musical associations.

nuance a slight or subtle change in something.

Glossary

Acknowledgements

Every effort has been made to trace the copyright holders of the material used in this book. If, however, any omissions have been made, we would be happy to rectify this. Please contact us at the address on the title page.

p6   Key skills information, taken from the QCA website (www.qca.org.uk).

p10   definition © The Collins English Dictionary

p24   quote from *Film Review* (The Guide) © The Guardian

p30   with reference to *The determinants of news photographs* © Hall, S. (1981) in *The Manufacture of News* (Sage Constable)

p61   *But Greenhouse gases are my only pleasure in life* cartoon, © John Longstaff

p64   *Hurricane Georges* map, © USA Today, reprinted with permission

p73   *Climate talks end in disarray* © The Observer, reprinted from front page (26th November 2000)

p77   quote from Human Cloning Foundation, *The Benefits of Human Cloning* 1998 Internet http://www.humancloning.org/benefits.htm

p81   *Why I'm happy to eat GM food* © The Evening Standard/Victor Sebestyen 10/8/00

p82   *What sort of world do we want to live in?* © Prince of Wales' website http://193.36.68.132/speeches/agriculture–01031999.html

p84   *Temperature changes graph* ©Hedley Centre, Met Office

p95   *Votes and seats of the major political parties in general elections since 1945* ©Macmillan, taken from Contemporary British Politics by NBill Coxall and Lynton Robins

p103   Structure of the NHS diagram, © Office of Health Economics, *Compendium of Health Statistics*, 1995

p105   *Spending on Health: International comparison diagram,* © Office of Health Economics, *Compendium of Health Statistics*, 1995

p106   definition © The Oxford English Dictionary

p106   *We all want to crack down on crime* cartoon © David Austin/The Guardian

p108-111   crime statistics taken from *Crime Concern report*

p109   Electrocution quote taken from Amnesty International website http://www.amnesty.org

p116   *Gross National Product estimates* © World Bank 1997/ ITU 1997/ UN 1996/ FAO 1997/ UNESCO 1997; *Shares of world consumption* © OUP 1998, taken from *World Resources* by The World Resources Institute, The United Nations Environmental Programme and The World Bank.